What We Can Learn from **Short Stories** and **Jokes**

SHIH WEI

What We Can Learn From Short Stories And Jokes

Copyright © 2023 by Shih Wei.

Paperback ISBN: 978-1-63812-431-3
Ebook ISBN: 9978-1-63812-432-0

All rights reserved. No part in this book may be produced and transmitted in any form or by any means, electronic, or mechanical, including photocopying, recording, or by any information storage and retrieval system, without permission in writing from the copyright owner.

The views expressed in this work are solely those of the author and do not necessarily reflect the views of the publisher hereby disclaims any responsibility for them.

Published by Pen Culture Solutions 02/02/2023

Pen Culture Solutions
1-888-727-7204 (USA)
1-800-950-458 (Australia)
support@penculturesolutions.com

Contents

Introduction vii

Chapter 1:   Appearance 1
Chapter 2:   Communications/Conversations 9
Chapter 3:   Greed 19
Chapter 4:   Helping One Another 23
Chapter 5:   Honesty 27
Chapter 6:   Impermanence 35
Chapter 7:   Ingenuity 37
Chapter 8:   Motivation 45
Chapter 9:   Perceptions/Viewpoints 47
Chapter 10: Pleasing Everybody 61
Chapter 11: Postponement 63
Chapter 12: Pride/Ego 65
Chapter 13: Struggles/Adversities 71
Chapter 14: Miscellaneous: Other Life Truths 77

Introduction

The shortest distance between a human being and truth is a story.
— Anthony de Mello —

Tell me a fact and I will learn. Tell me a truth and I will believe. But tell me a story and it will live in my heart forever.
— Native American proverb —

Stories and jokes can provide useful lessons if you look out for them.

Over the years, whenever I came across a captivating story or good joke which could teach us something or reveal some truth, I would think of how to tell it in my own words and draw an insightful lesson from it. This book is a compilation of 200 such stories and jokes. They are from various sources—books, jokes, the Internet, Aesop's Fables and ancient tales.

The stories/jokes have been carefully selected for their lessons. A short statement to illuminate a learning point follows each story/joke.

There are stories intended to encourage you. There are moral stories extolling certain values. There are also stories with lessons on motivation, human communications, perceptions, greed, pride, and the impermanent nature of all things. You will also learn not to be deceived by appearance and the peril of trying to please everybody. Seemingly innocent conversations between two children or two-liner jokes can also teach us a thing or two about human nature.

Enjoy the short stories and jokes. At the same time, see what you can learn from them.

Chapter 1

Appearance

1. The Man Who Has Forgotten His Wife's Name

Tommy, a young man, was visiting an elderly friend. The elderly man was in his eighties and had been married for more than fifty years. He was very loving towards his wife. He would always address her in endearing names—sweetheart, honey, my dearest, etc. Tommy was very impressed by his elderly friend's affection for his wife after so many years, and he wanted to know his secret. Looking around, making sure that his wife was not within earshot, the elderly man told Tommy, 'To tell you the truth, I forgot my wife's name more than ten years ago.'

Appearance

Lesson: **Things may not be what they appear to be. Appearance may well be different from reality.**

2. Two Bulls and the Piglet

There were two bulls and a piglet in a farm. The bulls toiled hard in the farm and were fed only with hay. On the other hand, the piglet was not given any work and was fed the best rich food. It grew fatter and fatter each day.

One day, the younger bull, who was envious of the piglet, expressed his bitterness to the elder bull. The elder, wiser bull replied, 'We don't have the full picture. We don't know what the outcome will be.'

True enough, soon afterwards the farmer's daughter was getting married. On the wedding day, the piglet was slaughtered for the day's ritual and the night's wedding feast.

Lesson: **Do not envy others. You do not have the full facts, and you do not know the final outcome.**

3. Two Apples

A father and his young daughter were walking along a park. They came across a fruit vendor. As the young girl liked apples, his father bought two. The young girl was holding one apple in each hand. She took a bite on an apple. His father asked her to share the apples by giving him one. The young girl took a bite at the other apple. Her father was very disappointed and wondered why her little girl could be so selfish and greedy. Just then, the girl stretched her hand to give his father an apple and said, 'Daddy, take this one. It is more juicy and sweeter.'

Lesson: At times, we can misunderstand the good intention of others.

4. Sincerity (A Persian tale)

A religious teacher was invited to feast with the king. He ate very little and then retired to say a long prayer. He did all these to impress the king.

When he reached home, the first thing he did was to take his dinner. His young son asked, 'Pa, didn't you have dinner with the king? Why are you eating again?'

The father answered, 'Yes, but I ate very little for a purpose.'

The very clever son quipped, 'Then you have to say your prayer again because you also did that for a purpose.'

Lesson: Do not think others cannot see through your intention. Be sincere.

5. Smuggling

There was a man who cycled across the border and brought along two sacks. The border guard asked what was in the sacks, and the man replied that they contained sand. The border guard checked and was satisfied that he was not smuggling any expensive items across and let him go. This happened daily for almost a year.

Then, the border guard retired. One day, he met the 'sand' man in a bar. The border guard asked the 'sand' man what he was trying to smuggle across the border as he was certain that the 'sand' man was trying to bring something illegally across the border. The 'sand' man replied, 'Bicycles.'

Appearance

Lesson: What is not obvious may be what you are looking for.

6. Who is Dumb?

A man liked to play a practical joke on a small boy to show that the boy was dumb. In front of few onlookers, he would ask the boy to pick a $2 note and a $5 note. The boy would always take the $2 note. One day, a kind man called the boy aside and advised him to take the $5 note as it had a higher value. The boy replied, 'If I take the $5 note, that fool will not play the joke on me anymore.'

Lesson: Sometimes you think you are smart and the other person is a fool. Actually, it is the other way round.

7. My Mother is at Home

A salesman saw a boy sitting on a porch in front of a house. The salesman asked him whether his mother was at home. The boy answered, 'Yes.' The salesman smilingly pressed the doorbell. No one answered. He asked the boy again. The boy again said, 'Yes.' The salesman pressed the doorbell another time. Again, no one responded.

The salesman then asked, 'Is your mother really at home?' The boy answered, 'She sure is. But I don't stay here.'

Lesson: Sometimes what is obvious may not be so.

8. Maybe

Once, there was a farmer whose horse ran away.

All his neighbours said to him, 'This is bad luck.'

The farmer replied, 'Maybe.'

The next day, his horse came back with two horses. 'This is good luck,' said his neighbours.

The farmer replied with his usual 'Maybe.'

The following day, the farmer's son rode on one of the new horses and fell down, breaking his leg.

The neighbours then said, 'This is bad luck.'

Again, the farmer replied, 'Maybe.' One week later, the government officials came to round up all able-bodied young men to fight in an impending war. The farmer's son was spared because of his injured leg.

Lesson: **In life what seems bad may turn out to be good and what appears good may be bad. Suspend judgement.**

9. The Ass in Lion's Clothing

An ass found a lion skin hung up to dry in a jungle. He wore it and walked into a nearby village. The villagers fled in fright on seeing the 'lion'. The ass was so delighted to see the villagers in such a frenzy state. In ecstasy, he raised his voice and brayed. The villagers gave him a good beating for causing them unwanted fright.

Lesson: **You can deceive others with your outward appearance but not so with your true essence inside you, which is often revealed when you open your mouth.**

10. A Bet

Appearance

Joe, a self-proclaimed know-all, placed a bet with Tom, who he thought was a fool.

Joe: I ask you a question. If you don't know or give the wrong answer, you pay me $5. You ask me a question. If I don't know or give the wrong answer, I pay you $50.

Tom readily agreed to the bet.

Joe: How many continents are there in the world?

Tom: I don't know.

Tom paid Joe $5.

Tom: Which animal has four legs in the daytime and three legs at night?

After pondering for ten minutes, Joe admitted that he did not know the answer and paid Tom $50.

Joe: And what is the answer?

Tom: I don't know.

Tom paid Joe $5.

Lesson: A smart person may not be clever; a fool may not be stupid.

11. Get Better Soon

Joe was a jolly retired man. He volunteered to entertain patients in hospitals. He would sing some funny songs (strumming along a guitar) and tell silly jokes to cheer up the patients.

One day, after entertaining an elderly man in a hospital, he said to the elderly patient when bidding good-bye, 'I hope you get better soon.' The man replied, 'I hope you get better too.'

Lesson: Sometimes you will be amazed at how people see you.

12. A Shipwreck

One fateful day, Bobby encountered a shipwreck. He was swept ashore alone on a small, uninhibited island. He prayed fervently for help but none came. Over a few days, he managed to build a small hut from the driftwood to protect him from the elements and cold at night. One day as he came back after looking for food, he found his hut on flames. He was so saddened and cried aloud to God. While still feeling down and desperate, watching his hut burning down, he heard the sound of a ship approaching the island.

Bobby was finally rescued. He also learnt that the ship came to rescue him when the crew saw the flame on the island.

Lesson: A blessing can come in disguise. A seemingly unfortunate event could well be something fortunate.

Chapter 2

Communications/ Conversations

1. Three Wishes

There was a poor, young couple. One day, a fairy appeared before them and announced that they would be granted three wishes.

Over dinner with only rice and potatoes, the wife lamented, 'How nice if we have sausages.' A plate of sausages appeared on the table.

The husband was angry at her for making such a simple wish and chided her, 'If you like sausages so much, let them grow from your nose.' Out came two long sausages from her nose.

She screamed, 'I don't want sausages.' Immediately, the sausages on the plate and her nose disappeared. They realised with sadness that their three wishes had been used up.

Lesson: Be careful with what you say. What you said may bring about something you do not want.

2. Two Swans and the Frog

Once, there were two swans and a frog living happily together in a lake. One day, the lake dried up. The swans decided to fly away to look for another lake. They wanted very much to take the frog along. But there was a problem — the frog could not fly. The frog then thought of a bright idea. He found a tree branch and asked his swan friends to bite each end. He himself bit at the centre. And off they flew. As they flew across a village, the villagers started to praise the ingenuity of the swans in flying with the frog. When the frog heard these, he could not resist to correct the villagers. He opened his mouth, 'It is . . .' and dropped to the ground.

Lesson: You do not always have to prove yourself right.

3. What Is the Problem?

A customer at a restaurant was complaining to a waitress, 'I can't drink my soup.'

Waitress: Sorry. I will let the captain know.

Captain: Let me check with the chef.

The chef came out and asked, 'What is the problem? Why can't you drink the soup?'

Customer: I don't have a spoon.

Lesson 1: Be specific in stating your problem so that others can understand it clearly.

Lesson 2: Find out what exactly the problem is before expending effort to resolve it.

4. A Circus

A lady tiger tamer was performing a stunning act in a circus. She put a sweet on her head and squatted down. A tiger removed the sweet from her head with its mouth. The audience was thrilled and applauded loudly. Just then, a man shouted, 'That's nothing. Anybody can do it.'

The lady performer shouted back scornfully, 'Can you do it?'

The man replied, 'Anybody can do it if a tiger can do it.'

Lesson 1: If a message has more than one meaning, we tend to interpret it based on what is obvious to us, even though it may not be the intended message.

Lesson 2: If a message has more than one meaning, it would be good to make it clearer to avoid misinterpretation.

5. A Lovely Couple

Wife to husband: Look at the lovely couple next door. Mr Tan kisses his wife every morning when he leaves for work. Why don't you do the same?

Husband: I would love to, but I don't know her well enough.

Lesson: It is better not to leave room for ambiguity. An ambiguous statement is one which can be interpreted in more than one way.

6. The Frog and the Cock

One day, a frog asked a cock, 'Why is it that when you crow, everybody wakes up and gets into action, but when I croak, nobody pays attention?'

The cock replied, 'I crow for a purpose, but you croak throughout the day for no rhyme or reason.'

Lesson: When you talk when necessary, you will be listened to. When you talk incessantly, you will be ignored.

7. A Sparkling Diamond

One day, Robert was walking along a street when he saw an injured cat, apparently fallen into a drain, trying to climb up. He rescued the cat. The cat turned into a genie and offered to grant Robert three wishes for being so kind.

'Make me a millionaire.' was Robert's first wish.

'Granted. I have credited 5 million into your bank account,' replied the genie.

'Give me a big house.' was the next wish.

'You also have this,' replied the genie.

'Make me irresistible to women.' was Robert's last wish.

The genie turned him into a sparkling diamond.

Lesson: In communications, it is important not to assume that the other party has the same understanding as you. It is better to be specific than sorry.

8. Saying Grace at Dinner

Alice invited her friends for dinner at her home. She asked her five-year-old son, Johnny, to say grace.

'I don't know what to say,' Johnny protested.

'Just say what you heard mummy said,' his father answered.

Johnny bowed his head, closed his eyes, and said, 'Lord, why on earth did I invite all these people for dinner?'

Lesson: Be careful with what you say in front of children.

9. An English Lesson

Teacher: Jane, give me a sentence beginning with I.

Jane: I is …..

Teacher, interrupting: No, Jane, it is wrong to say I is. You always say I am.

Jane: All right. I am the ninth letter in the alphabet.

Lesson: Wait till the other person has finished her sentence before you correct her. Do not jump to correction.

10. Mugging

A man met two muggers on a lonely street one night. He fought hard and struggled until they gave up. The muggers found a $1 coin in his pants. One of the muggers was amused and asked why he had fought so hard for a dollar.

The man replied, 'Gee, I thought you all were after my $500 in my shoe.'

Lesson: Do not open your mouth unnecessarily.

11. A Therapy Session

Patient: Doctor, please help me. Everybody says I am a liar.

Therapist: I can't believe that.

Lesson: Sometimes we inadvertently say things we should not say.

12. Nothing Good to Say

James was a hardworking and busy manager. He had so much work that left him no time to tidy his desk, which was cluttered with files, stationery, documents and other papers.

One day, his boss walked by and, seeing the chaotic state of James's desk, commented, 'I hope your mind is not as cluttered as your desk.' That evening after work, James stayed back and cleared his desk.

The next morning, his boss walked by again and, seeing the desk cleared of all items, commented, 'I hope your mind is not as empty as your desk.'

Lesson: Some people just seem to have nothing good to say on anything.

13. An Unexpected Question

Teacher: Good, Tom. You finally raised your hand to ask a question.

Tom: Thank you, teacher. May I go to the toilet?

Lesson: Do not assume and jump to conclusions.

14. Going for a Haircut

A man went to the barber. As soon as the barber wrapped a cover sheet over him, the customer said, 'Before we start, I know the weather is terribly hot. I am interested in neither sports nor politics. I don't gamble, buy shares and I don't have children. OK, now you can proceed.'

The barber said, 'Sir, if you don't mind, I can concentrate better if you talk less.'

Lesson: Do not assume everybody likes to talk to you.

15. The Lion with a Bad Breath (Aesop's Fables)

Once, there was a lion with a terrible bad breath. He asked the deer whether he had a bad breath. The deer truthfully answered, 'Yes.' The lion could not stand the truth and ate up the deer. The lion then asked the wolf the same question. The wolf answered, 'Not at all.' The lion could not stand the flattery and ate up the wolf. He then asked the fox. The fox answered, 'I had a flu and blocked nose today. So sorry, I cannot tell.' The fox was spared.

Lesson: Sometimes it is best not to express any opinion.

16. A Surgery

Kim was running frantically out of the operating theatre. As he was descending a flight of stairs, he met the head nurse who was surprised to see him in such a state.

Head Nurse: Sir, you look like you are escaping from the operating theatre. What is the problem?

Kim: The nurse said, 'It is a simple operation. It will turn out all right. Don't worry.'

Head Nurse: She was just trying to comfort you.

Kim: But she was not talking to me. She was talking to the young surgeon.

Lesson: The same message has different meanings when directed at different people.

17. A Timeout

Wife: Since our children are in school camp, shall we go out and have some fun tonight?

Husband: Sure. Good idea. If you come back before me, please leave the balcony light on.

Lesson: This is another story reminding us not to be ambiguous in our communications with others.

18. A Forgetful Patient

Larry, an elderly man, went to consult a psychiatrist for his poor memory.

Larry: Doctor, I forget things very quickly.

Psychiatrist: How quickly?

Larry: How quickly, what?

Lesson: Sometimes you do not need a direct answer to get the answer.

19. Stamp Collection

John was talking to his friend, Tom, about Toms' application for a job as a postman.

John: I thought you were quite sure that you could get the job.

Tom: I was. Maybe, it was because I told them that my biggest hobby is collecting stamps.

Lesson: Be discreet in what you tell others.

20. Fools

Fred: I agree with what one philosopher said — 'Fools are always so certain of themselves, and the wise people are full of doubts.'

Willy: Are you sure?

Fred: Certainly sure.

Lesson: **Sometimes we inadvertently said something about ourselves which we did not mean.**

21. Foolish Advice

Mr Huang was visiting his family doctor. As he was familiar with the doctor, he started a casual conversation.

Huang: Before I came here, I went to consult a fortune teller and a palm reader.

Doctor: And what foolish advice they gave you?

Huang: They both advised me to come to see you.

Lesson: **Do not condemn too soon.**

Chapter 3

Greed

1. A Greedy Dog (Aesop's Fables)

One day, a dog found a big bone. He was so delighted. He carried it with his mouth and looked for a shady place to enjoy his meal. While walking, he came across a lake and saw another dog with a bigger bone. He wanted the bigger bone too and barked at the other dog. He dropped the bone into the lake. Only then did he realise it was his reflection. He walked away dejected and regretted his greediness.

Lesson: Be content with what you have. Otherwise, you may even lose what you have.

2. The Fox and the Dog (Aesop's Fables)

One evening, a fox caught a dog. As the fox was about to eat the dog, the dog pleaded, 'Don't eat me yet. I am just a skinny dog. You will be eating more bones than meat. I am going to a grand wedding feast. You can eat me after that when I will be fatter. I will surely pass by this way again on my way home after the wedding dinner.' The fox imagined a more juicy meat and thought it was a good idea to have a delicious meal later. The fox let the dog go. He waited and waited for the dog the whole night.

Lesson: As often said, 'Opportunity knocks but once.' Missed opportunities seldom come back. Do not be greedy. 'A bird in your hand is worth two on the bush.'

3. Free Land

A very wealthy man offered free land to a farmer. The farmer would get all the land he walked starting from sunrise but he had to return to the starting point by sunset. The farmer started to walk promptly at sunrise. He walked and walked, hoping to get as much free land as possible. He continued to walk until late afternoon. By then, greed had got him so far that he had little time to return to the starting point by sunset. He ran as fast as he could but still did not manage to make it. He collapsed and died before reaching the starting point.

Lesson: Do not be greedy. It is good to want to achieve more and get more things in life. But we have to balance it with knowing when it is enough.

4. A Greedy Rich Man

Hamid was a rich businessman. He was a miser and paid his workers very little. He was also very greedy and would not hesitate to use deceitful ways to make more money. Once, he lost a bag containing fifty gold coins. It was devastating to him. He looked and asked around.

A little boy found the bag and handed it over to his father. His father happened to be a worker of Hamid. He, being an honest man, returned the bag to his boss. On seeing the bag, Hamid, instead of being thankful, quickly thought of a way to cheat the poor, honest worker. Hamid insisted that the bag contained 100 gold coins and demanded that the man return the missing coins.

The case went up to the court. The man told the judge that had he wanted to steal the fifty gold coins, he would not have returned the bag to Hamid at all.

The judge asked Hamid, 'Are you sure that your bag contains 100 gold coins?'

Hamid answered confidently, 'My Lord, I am very sure.'

The judge then said, 'Then this bag definitely does not belong to you.'

He ordered the man to keep the bag with the fifty gold coins.

Lesson: You may end up losing when you try to cheat others.

5. A Jar of Nuts

Little John saw a jar of nuts on the table. He put his hand inside and grasped a fistful of nuts. He could not get his hand out from the jar and began to cry loudly. His mother came out and said to him calmly, 'John, it is simple. Just let go of all the nuts you cling on and pick up only a few.'

Lesson: **If you go after too much of something, you may end up getting nothing.**

6. A Car Broke Down

One day, Mary's car was stalled in the middle of a quiet road as it ran out of petrol. Fortunately, two strong young men passed by. Mary requested them to push her car to a petrol station. The two men readily helped her. After pushing the car for about 200 metres, the men were relieved to see a petrol station. But Mary did not turn into the station. Mary shouted to the two men, 'This petrol station does not give trading stamps. I usually go to the station about 500 metres further from here.'

Lesson: **Some people are never satisfied and grateful with the help rendered to them.**

Chapter 4

Helping One Another

1. The Donkey and the Mule (Aesop's Fables)

There was a man who had a donkey and a mule. One day, they were travelling to another city. The man put all the load on the donkey and spared the mule. At first, the donkey was able to bear the load. But when walking up a steep cliff, he found it too hard to bear. He pleaded with the mule for help. The mule, being unhelpful, refused to help the donkey. After treading for a while, the donkey could not bear the load any longer. He collapsed and died. As they have to continue travelling, the master transferred all the load from the donkey to the mule. The mule regretted that he had not extended a helping hand to the donkey.

Lesson: You never know, by helping others you are helping yourself.

2. Balloons

During a seminar, the trainer conducted an activity. All fifty participants were given a balloon. Each of them wrote his/her name on the balloon. The trainer then put all the balloons in another room. He instructed all the participants to go to the room and get his/her own balloon without helping one another. After three minutes, none of the participants found his/her balloon. The trainer then asked the participants to pick a balloon at random and give it to the person whose name appeared on the balloon. Less than three minutes, all participants found their balloons.

The trainer then shared the lesson learnt. He said, 'The balloons represent happiness. Everybody is busy finding one's own happiness but could not find it until one helps another person to find his/her happiness.'

Lesson: Do not just look for your own happiness. Give it to others and you will find yours.

3. The Long Spoon

A reporter was sent for a study trip to heaven and hell. One thing he reported was that both places served the same food during meals and that the residents were provided each with a long spoon. In heaven, everyone enjoyed the meal as they fed each other. In hell, all were starving even though there was enough food. They were trying to feed themselves with the long spoon which could not reach their mouths.

Lesson: There are things which an individual cannot do by himself/herself. Helping one another is the only way to achieve them.

4. Asking for Help

Little Tom was trying to remove a big rock in his garden with all his might. The rock did not budge a bit. His father asked him whether he had used all his strength.

Tom replied, 'Yes, I used all my strength.'

His father replied, 'No, you didn't. You have not asked me to help.'

Lesson: It takes strength to ask for help.

Chapter 5

Honesty

1. The Donkey and a Sack of Salt (Aesop's Fables)

A man was travelling with his donkey. The donkey was carrying a sack of salt. While crossing a bridge, the donkey accidentally fell into a river. After getting up, they resumed their journey. The donkey found that the load he was carrying had become lighter (as some salt dissolved in the river). The next day, he intentionally fell into the river. The same thing happened again the subsequent day. The day after, the man changed the sack of salt into a sack of cloth. The donkey fell into the river again. This time he found the load to be heavier as the cloth absorbed the water.

Lesson: You cannot cheat people all the time. One day, your trick will be uncovered and it may be your turn to be tricked instead.

2. The Princess's Hair Clips

Once upon a time, there was a king who had six beautiful daughters. All the princesses had long, lovely hair. The king gave each of them 100 hair clips made of the finest and rarest gems. One day, the eldest princess discovered that she had lost one hair clip. She stole one from the second princess. When the second princess found out that one of her hair clips was missing, she stole one from the third princess. The same thing happened to the other princesses. The youngest princess was saddened when she realised that one hair clip had gone missing. But she had no thoughts of stealing from her sisters. One day, a handsome prince from a neighbouring kingdom came with a missing hair clip. He told the king that a dove had dropped the hair clip on his balcony, and he knew that it belonged to one of the princesses. The youngest princess claimed the missing hair clip and went off with the handsome prince, much to the regrets of all her sisters.

Lesson: It pays to be honest.

3. A Chicken Seller

Lily went to the market to buy a chicken during the closing hours. The seller picked up his last chicken from below the stall and put on the weighing machine. Lily asked for a bigger one. The seller pretended to put back the chicken and take another one. He put the same chicken on the weighing machine with part of his hand slightly on the machine. Lily then said, 'OK, I'll take both.'

Lesson: Telling lies may lead to an embarrassing situation.

4. An Unexpected Award

Benny was the most capable and trusted worker of Sam, a successful builder of houses. One day, Benny decided it was time to retire after working for almost 50 years. He informed Sam of his plan to retire. Sam was saddened that he would be losing a very good helper. He requested Benny to help him build one last house. Benny thought that since he would be retiring, there was no need to put in his best effort. He slacked in the job, cut corners, and even cheated by buying inferior materials. When the house was completed, Sam presented the key to Benny as a gift for his outstanding long service. Benny received the award with regrets and a sense of shame when he should have received it with pride had he put in his usual best effort and honesty.

Lesson: **Whatever you do, you do it to yourself.**

5. I Am Watching over Me (A tale From Ancient India)

Once, there was a master with twelve disciples who were graduating. He had a beautiful daughter, and he would like her to marry one of his disciples. All his disciples were interested in his daughter. The master devised a plan to find out which disciple is worthy of his daughter.

He gathered his disciples and told them, 'I am finding a husband for my daughter among you all. But I could not decide. I also do not have much money to throw a wedding banquet and to give the dowry. I shall now have a contest to find my son-in-law. For one week starting tonight, go to the villages in the middle of the night and steal as many things as you can when no one is watching.' The disciples were shocked that their master told them to steal as he was an upright man. Nevertheless, they followed his instructions.

After a week, the master gathered his disciples to announce the result. He carried a record on the list of things his disciples had stolen. One disciple stood out. He had not stolen anything. When the master

Honesty

asked him why, he answered, 'You told us to steal when no one was watching.'

The master interrupted, 'Yes, but everyone was sleeping in the middle of the night and no one was watching.'

The disciple continued, 'Whenever I was about to steal, I saw myself watching over me. That is why I did not steal anything.'

The master was very pleased with this disciple and announced that he was the winner. He then told the other disciples, 'Go and return what you have stolen. Do not worry. You will not be punished. The villagers actually knew my plan.'

Lesson: A wrong action seen by someone is also wrong when no one sees it.

6. A Promise

Bala had just bought a handsome and elegant horse in the marketplace. On his way back, he met a terrific hurricane. The storm was blowing him away and his horse was also struggling. Bala earnestly prayed for his safety and promised to sell the horse and give the money to the poor if his prayer was answered. Soon after he uttered the prayer, the storm subsided.

A week later, with his conscience pricking him, Bala went to the marketplace to sell his horse. He brought along a goose. He told a potential buyer that he would have to buy the goose along with the horse.

'How much?' the buyer asked.

Bala replied, 'The horse is 10 rupees and the goose is 1,000 rupees.'

Lesson: Some people are cunning and calculative and will find ways to gain an advantage.

7. A Dishonest Salesman

Once, there were two door-to-door salesmen in a small town. Kenny was a dishonest person who would take every opportunity to cheat on people and maximise his gains. Larry was kind-hearted and was always honest in his dealings.

One day, Kenny knocked on a door to sell his wares. An elderly lady opened the door. Her little granddaughter was with her. Kenny displayed a few colourful plastic bracelets. The little girl was attracted by the bracelets and pestered her grandmother to buy one. The elderly lady politely apologised to Kenny that she was poor and could not afford to buy anything from him. As Kenny was about to leave, the little girl rushed to her room and brought out an old metal coin covered with dust. She asked Uncle Kenny whether she could exchange it with a bracelet. Kenny removed the dust from the metal and immediately knew that it was made of real gold. At that moment, Kenny recalled that he still had a few inferior quality bracelets at home. He wanted to exchange one of those with the gold coin. So he told the little girl that the metal piece was worthless and left, having in mind to come back again with the cheaper bracelets. He was thinking that they would surely be more than happy to trade the 'worthless' coin with any bracelets.

Soon after Kenny left, Larry knocked at the door. Larry also showed them some bracelets. The little girl again tried to trade the metal coin with a colourful bracelet. Larry took the metal coin and exclaimed, 'This is real gold. You can have all the bracelets and all my earnings for the day in exchange for it.' The elderly lady and the little girl were delighted.

Then, Kenny came back. When the elderly lady opened the door, Kenny said, 'I changed my mind, and thinking that your little granddaughter wants a bracelet so much, I am willing to exchange it with the worthless metal coin.' The elderly lady then told him what happened.

Kenny, betrayed by his own dishonesty and greed, walked away dejected.

Lesson: You do not always gain by being dishonest and greedy.

8. A Repentant Thief

Once, there was a king who visited a prison. All the prisoners, except one, maintained their innocence and insisted that they had been unjustly imprisoned. One repentant prisoner confessed that he had committed a theft.

The king exclaimed, 'Throw this thief out. He will corrupt the other innocents here!'

Lesson: It is never wrong to admit a wrong.

9. A Jug of Wine

A rich village chief planned to throw a feast for the village heads to celebrate the New Year. He told the village elders that he would pay for the food and entertainment but they would each have to contribute a jug of wine.

One village elder thought that it would not make any difference if he would mix the wine with water. On the day of the feast, as the village elders walked to the village chief's garden, they poured their jug of wine into a large clay pot.

After eating the sumptuous food, the servants served the wine. All the guests tried to avoid looking at the village chief and drank the wine as though it were the best wine in the world. Everyone had brought along a jug of diluted wine.

Lesson: Ponder carefully the consequence of a situation if everyone else thinks like you.

10. The Emperor and the Seed

There was an emperor who was getting old and wanted to look for a successor. As he had no children, he planned to choose his successor from among the kingdom's top ten scholars. He gathered the scholars and gave them each a pot and a seed.

The emperor instructed, 'Bring back the seed and grow the plant. Next year at this time, bring your plant back. The one who can grow the best plant will be the next king.' The scholars were, of course, very excited.

One year later on the appointed time, the scholars came back. All, except one named Rong, carried a large plant. They were very eager to show the king their plant after one year of effort in caring for it. Rong brought back the same pot and seed and explained to the king that the seed could not grow.

To everyone's surprise, the king embraced Rong and declared him as his successor. The king then addressed the gathering, 'One year ago, I gave you all a seed. The seed had been boiled and could not grow.

As all of you are smart, I do not look for cleverness in choosing my successor. I look for someone who is honest and Rong is the one.'

Lesson: Your integrity is under test.

11. Stealing Pencils

George was an eight-year-old kid. One day, his mother received a call from his teacher. The teacher informed her that George had stolen a pencil from a classmate. George's mother was furious and gave him a good scolding when he came back from school. At the end of a long lecture, the mother said to George, 'Remember, when you need pencils, dad can always bring back some from work.'

Lesson: It is easy to practise double standards. And this can confuse a child.

Chapter 6

Impermanence

1. The Last Call

A group of children were playing at a beach. They were making sandcastles, zealously guarding their masterpieces, sometimes envious of each other's. Evening came, and it was time to go home. Their mothers called them to return. The children stood up and ran towards their mummies, stepping over the sandcastles they painstakingly built.

Lesson: Life is impermanent. When death beckons, you too have to leave everything behind and go. Life is like a balloon — impermanent and empty. No matter how colourful and beautiful a balloon is, all burst balloons look alike.

2. 'This, too, shall pass' (A Sufi story)

Once, there was a king who was torn by the ups and downs of life. He commissioned a man known for his wisdom to devise a way for him to get out of this frustration. He would pay any price for it. A few weeks later, the wise man presented the king with a golden ring. The king was furious at first. The wise man then explained the inscription beneath the ring which read, 'This, too, shall pass.' He advised the king to look at this inscription whenever he was affected by the vicissitudes of life and be reminded of the fleeting nature of everything. The king was very pleased with the ring.

Lesson: All things are fleeting. The most glorious moment as well as the darkest time will pass.

3. A Class Photo

It was the last day of the year for a primary one class. The form teacher gave each student a group class photo.

The teacher said, 'Keep and treasure the photo. One day, you may be telling your children, 'Look, this is Dr Singh, the cleverest kid in class. This is Ricky, my best friend. He is now a director of a company.'

A boy from behind, pointing his finger on the teacher on the photo, said, 'And this is our form teacher, Madam Jessica. She is now gone.'

Lesson: This story is a powerful reminder of our mortality. As someone has observed — 'Photos last longer than people.'

Chapter 7

Ingenuity

1. Someone Hiding Under My Bed

Lester went to see a psychiatrist because he was always thinking someone was hiding under his bed whenever he was on it. The psychiatrist said that he would cure him completely with six counselling sessions at $200 per session. Lester said he would consider it and left the clinic.

One month later, Lester and the psychiatrist bumped into each other. The psychiatrist asked Lester why he had not come back. Lester replied, 'I am now completely cured. In any case, you are expensive. My fishmonger advised me to cut off the legs of my bed, and he arranged a carpenter friend to do it for $50.'

Lesson: There is usually a cheaper and more effective solution.

2. One Wish (A Jewish tale)

Once, there was a blind, childless and poor man. He and his wife toiled hard but never complained. One day, an angel appeared and announced that God would grant him one and only one wish. The man could not decide what to wish for. He requested the angel to give him a day to think about it.

(Remember, the man is blind, childless and poor. What will he wish for?)

The next day, the man met the angel again. He stated his wish — 'I wish to see my children eating off golden plates.' His wish was granted.

Lesson: When confronted with a seemingly difficult decision, think harder. A perfect solution may be around the corner.

3. A Witty Dog

A dog strayed into a jungle. He was spotted by a hungry lion. The lion was about to pounce on him. The dog panicked and saw some bones nearby. He said loudly, 'Mmm, that was the best lion meat I have tasted.' The lion was shocked and abruptly stopped. He thought to himself that the dog might be tougher than his look. The lion then turned away quickly.

A monkey on a tree saw what was happening. The monkey thought that he could benefit by telling the lion what had happened. The lion then told the monkey to jump onto his back and they would both go to look for that cunning dog.

When the dog saw them coming, he shouted loudly to the monkey, 'I told you to get me a lion an hour ago and you only come now!' The lion quickly threw the monkey down and ran as far as he could.

Lesson: Do not panic in an emergency. Your quick wit may rescue you.

4. The Eighteenth Horse

There was a rich merchant who had three children. He had a will stating with precision how to share his land, money, gold and horses among the three children. After his death, the children had no problem in following his will, except they did not know how to distribute his seventeen horses in accordance with the will, which was 1/2, 1/3 and 1/9 respectively. They then approached a wise old man who was a good friend of their late father. The wise man gave them his one horse. They divided the eighteen horses accordingly to 9 + 6 + 2. This added up to 17 horses. The wise old man got back his horse.

Lesson: With some thoughts, you can help others solve their problems without giving up what you have.

5. A One-Legged, One-Eyed King

There was a king who was born with one leg and one eye. One day, he summoned the best painters in the kingdom to his palace. Pointing to a row of beautiful portraits of past kings, he offered the painters a great reward to paint an excellent portrait of himself so that future generations could remember him. None, except one painter, dared to take the challenge. They were fearful that the king would be angry if they could not produce a beautiful portrait due to the king's physical defects.

Ingenuity

All present waited in suspense for a few hours for the painter to complete the king's portrait. When completed, the painter showed his work to the king and all present. The king was very pleased.

The portrait showed the king riding on a horse. It showed one side of the king — the side with the leg. It also showed the king aiming an arrow with one eye closed.

Lesson: Everyone likes to have his/her weak spots covered.

6. A Black and a White Pebble

Once, there was a humble businessman who owed an old, unscrupulous loan shark lots of money. After several deadlines, the businessman was still not able to return the money. Standing on his garden on a path full of pebbles, the loan shark offered the businessman and his daughter a deal.

The loan shark said to the businessman's daughter, 'I am going to prepare two bags. One contains a black pebble and the other a white pebble. If you pick the bag with the black pebble, I will write off your father's debt but you have to marry me. If you pick the bag with the white pebble, I will also write off your father's debt and you do not have to marry me.'

The loan shark then proceeded to put a pebble into the bag. The daughter saw the loan shark putting a black pebble in both bags. The quick-witted lady did not expose the loan shark. Instead, she proceeded to pick a bag. As she took out the pebble, she 'accidentally' dropped it among the other pebbles.

She then apologised, 'How clumsy am I to drop the pebble. But if you look at the pebble in the other bag, you will know which pebble I picked.'

The loan shark had no choice but to honour the deal.

Lesson: With some creative and fast thinking, a problematic situation can be turned into an opportunity.

7. The King and His Three Sons

There was a king who was looking for his successor from among his three sons. He devised a plan to test the ingenuity of his sons. He gave each of them five pieces of gold and asked them to think of a way to fill up an empty room in the palace. The winner would be the one with the best idea and spent the least.

The eldest son went to the market and bought a load of cotton. In addition, he paid labourers to transport the cotton and fill up the room. The second son hired labourers to gather dried leaves and bring them back to fill up the room. The youngest son spent only a few silvers to buy a candle and a match to light up the room.

Guess who the king picked as his successor?

Lesson: Do not just think of things.

8. A Flawed Ruby

There was a king who was very fond of his priceless and beautiful ruby. He would admire it several times a day. One day, to his horror, he discovered a crack line on the ruby. He was devastated. He ordered his officials to look for the best jeweller to mend the crack. None of them dared to attempt for fear of damaging the ruby further.

One old, retired jeweller took up the challenge. He carved a beautiful rose with the crack line as the stem, making the ruby even more appealing to the king. The king was very pleased.

Lesson: You can turn your flaws into something useful.

9. The King Picked His Successor

Once, there was a king who devised a plan to pick his successor from among his four sons. He organised a big feast in a large room. He then let in four wild, hungry dogs. All his sons, except one, ran away. That son threw some food on the wild dogs. The dogs, and he himself, then enjoyed the feast.

Lesson: Running away from problems will not solve them.

10. The Princess and Her Suitors

There was once a beautiful princess. She was very good at horse racing. So far, no one had beaten her in this sport. When the king arranged to find her a husband, her only condition was that the successful suitor must beat her in horse racing. Several suitors failed to succeed.

One handsome prince was determined to marry the princess. He sent a messenger to gather information about the princess. The messenger reported that the princess had a weak spot for apples. She could not resist eating big red apples. On the day of the race, the prince arranged for food stalls to be placed at few locations along the way. The stall displayed prominently big red apples. Sure enough, the princess stopped to have a taste of the tempting apples. The smart prince then won the race and the princess's heart.

Lesson: One of the basic principles of Sun Tzu's The Art of War is to 'know yourself and your enemy'. In order to overcome an enemy (or a problem), understand more about the opponent.

11. Giving a Ride

Richard was a flamboyant young man. One stormy night, he was driving his new two-seat sports car. Along a remote, quiet road, he passed by a bus stop and saw three persons. One was a frail old lady looking as though she needed medical attention, and one was his old friend who once saved his life. The last one was a pretty young girl whom he very much would like to befriend. He could only offer a ride to one of them. He would very much like to offer the young girl a ride. But his conscience told him that she was the least deserving.

What would Richard do? A bright idea struck him. He passed the car key to his old friend and asked him to send the old lady to the hospital. And he waited for the bus with the young lady.

Lesson: Ingenuity can put you out of a dilemma.

Chapter 8

Motivation

1. The Sun and the Wind (Aesop's Fables)

Once, the sun and wind were debating who was stronger. They saw a man with an overcoat passing by. The wind suggested that whoever could make the man take off his overcoat within a shorter time would be the winner. The wind started to blow hard. The stronger he blew, the harder the man held onto his overcoat. The wind gave up. The sun began to shine on the man. The man could not stand the heat and took off his overcoat willingly.

Lesson: It is better to make a person want to do something than force him/her to do so.

2. A Property Agent

Motivation

Joseph, a property agent, was utterly dismayed. He was close to closing a lucrative deal but it failed eventually. When discussing the matter with his manager, he tried to rationalise and said, 'I can bring a horse to a well, but I cannot make it drink.'

The manager retorted, 'Who asked you to make the horse drink? Make it thirsty.'

Lesson: Like the previous story, make a person want to do something rather than force him/her to do so.

3. Taking Pills

Doctor: Take the yellow pill with a glass of water every morning after breakfast. Take the red pill with a glass of water after lunch. Take the blue pill with a glass of water before sleep. Remember to take all the pills with a glass of water, understand?

Patient: Yes, doctor. By the way, what exactly is my problem?

Doctor: You are not drinking enough water.

Lesson: Sometimes we need to devise a way to make someone do something.

Chapter 9

Perceptions/Viewpoints

1. The Other Side

A man was walking along a riverbank, thinking how to get across. He saw another man on the opposite bank.

'Hey, friend,' he shouted, 'how can I get to the other side?'

'You're already at the other side,' came the reply.

Lesson: We all have different perspectives. When it comes to viewpoints, there is no right or wrong.

2. The Rooster and a Diamond (Aesop's Fables)

Perceptions/Viewpoints

One day, a rooster was feeding himself with grains. He took a hard, shining stone and split it out. At that moment, the farmer's wife came out and screamed. 'Oh, my diamond! Luckily, he did not swallow it.' The rooster wondered, 'Why are diamonds so precious to people? To me they are useless.'

Lesson: What is valuable to you may not be valuable to others. What you like may not be the same as what others like.

3. Caution and Cowardice

A college teacher asked her class to explain the difference between caution and cowardice. One perceptive student answered, 'Caution is when you are afraid, and cowardice is when others are afraid.'

Lesson: We tend to find faults in others and justify our own.

4. Opportunity or Problem

Many years ago, a shoe manufacturer sent a sales executive to a remote village in another country to explore marketing opportunities there. On seeing that the tribe there did not wear shoes, he telegrammed back, 'Bad. People here do not wear shoes. No market.' He then packed and went home. Weeks later, a competitor also sent its sales executive to the same place. This time, the sales executive telegrammed back, 'Great. Expand production. People here do not wear shoes.'

Lesson: Same situation, but one sees it as a problem while another sees an opportunity. Perspective makes the difference. In fact, it is said that perspective is reality.

5. The Monkey in a Bar

John was just served a glass of beer in a bar. Soon after, a monkey appeared from nowhere and snatched away the glass. John asked the pub owner who the monkey belonged to. The pub owner told John that the monkey belonged to the pianist.

John walked to the pianist and asked, 'Do you know your monkey stole my beer?'

The pianist replied, 'No, but if you hum it, I can play it.'

Lesson: Some people just cannot see your problems because of their limited viewpoints and experiences.

6. A Cramped House

Once, there was a man who was depressed because he felt that his in-laws staying with him were taking up too much space in his house. He went to see a teacher who advised him to put all his chickens, dogs and sheep in his house. He did as told. After a while, he went to the teacher again complaining that his problem had got worse. This time, his teacher advised him to put back those animals outside. He then realised that he had so much space in his house.

Lesson: Count your blessings. While you do your best to improve things, remember also that things could have been worse.

7. As You Expected

There was a newcomer to a town. He asked an old-timer how the people were in the new town. The old-timer asked him back about the people in his town where he came from. 'They were selfish, unhelpful and arrogant,' replied the newcomer.

Perceptions/Viewpoints

'Same here,' replied the old-timer.

Another newcomer came to the town. He asked the same old-timer the same question. Again, the old-timer asked him back the question. 'They were kind, friendly and pleasant,' replied the second newcomer.

'Same here,' replied the old-timer.

A merchant nearby overheard the conversation. He asked the old-timer why he had given two opposite replies to the same question.

The old-timer replied philosophically, 'All of us carry their world in their heart.'

Lesson: **People seem to behave as you expect them to. If you think the world is hostile, you will experience it that way. If you think the world is friendly, you will experience it that way too. As Jon Kabat-Zinn said in his book's title, *Wherever you go, there you are.***

8. A Worm in an Apple

Mary: This morning, when I was biting an apple, I found a worm inside. Hard luck.

Lucy: You were lucky that you did not find half a worm inside.

Lesson: **Things could be worse.**

9. Twin Brothers

Joe has twin sons. Apart from resemblance in look, the twin brothers are opposite in all other aspects. One is a hopeless pessimist and the other an impossible optimist. On a birthday, Joe put some toy gadgets in the pessimist boy's room and a little pile of horse manure in the optimist boy's room.

On passing by the pessimist's room, Joe observed that his son was sad and asked him why. The boy lamented a list of sorrows — his friends would be jealous, he might not understand the instructions, he had to ensure that he had batteries, the toys might be faulty or lost.

Joe then walked over to the optimist's room and found him happy and excited. He wondered why. The boy replied, 'There must be a pony nearby!'

Lesson: **One's outlook in life will make a world of difference.**

10. A Lake and a Fountain

In a beautiful park, there was a lake and a fountain.

The lake was envious of the fountain. The lake thought, 'How I wish I were a fountain. The fountain is always so lively, can sing and dance well, and wins the admiration of so many people. Whereas I am so plain and dull, and people just ignore me as they pass by.'

On the other hand, the fountain was envious of the lake. The fountain thought, 'How I wish I were a lake. The lake is so blissful. People just stroll by the lake and enjoy its serenity. The lake has it so easy. I am so tired and weary having to perform continuously to entertain the people.'

Lesson: **Theodore Roosevelt said, 'Comparison is the thief of joy.' Do not compare. The grass on the other side is always greener. This is true for both sides.**

11. A Long Married Life

An elderly couple was interviewed during their sixtieth anniversary.

Interviewer asking the wife: Does your husband have any faults?

Wife: Many. As many as the stars.

Interviewer: Any good points?

Wife: Only one like the sun.

Interviewer: Then why are you able to stay with him for sixty years?

Wife: Because when the sun shines, the stars disappear.

Lesson: **It all depends on where you look. Look at the good points of a person.**

12. Small Stuff (A Jewish humor)

A grandmother brought her only grandson to a beach to play. Suddenly, a strong wave came and swept the boy away. The grandmother was shocked and pleaded to God. She prayed, 'Oh, God, please, please bring back my boy.' Her plea was answered. Another wave from the other direction swept back her grandson. The grandmother quickly carried the boy and looked up, 'Oh, God, he was wearing a hat.'

Lesson: **We can be very petty in life and have no sense of what is truly important.**

13. A 'Worm' Story

Story A: A speaker was speaking on the Evils of Alcohols. At the end of the speech, he gave a demonstration. He placed two containers filled with some water. One contained pure water and the other was diluted with alcohol. He then placed a worm on the container with pure water. The worm wriggled out and slowly climbed out of the container. Next, he put another worm into the other container, and the worm died.

'What is the moral of the story?' the speaker asked. He continued, 'The moral of the story is, alcohol kills.'

Someone behind the room shouted, 'The moral of the story is if you drink alcohol, you will never have worms.'

Story B: A teacher was trying to teach her class the virtue of acting fast and not procrastinating in order to succeed in life. The teacher concluded, 'Remember, the early bird catches the worm.'

Little Monica raised her hand and asked timidly, 'What about the early worm that was caught by the bird?'

Lesson: There are usually two sides to a story.

14. True Value

Once, there was a man who was lost in a desert. He almost ran out of food supply. Suddenly, he spotted a bag sack. Hoping that it would contain some grains, he opened it. He saw a bag of pearls.

Ordinarily, a sack of pearls was worth more than a sack of grains. However, the pearls were of no use to the man.

Lesson: If a thing is truly valuable, its value will not change regardless of the situation.

15. 'Mary, Mary'

The head of a mental hospital went round and toured the hospital. He saw a man kept swinging his body back and forth and mumbling, 'Mary, Mary.' The psychiatrist in attendance explained that Mary was the woman who had jilted her. As he went further, he saw another man who kept hitting his hands on the wall and crying out, 'Mary, Mary.'

The head asked, 'Is Mary also this man's problem?'

The psychiatrist replied, 'Mary is his wife.'

Lesson: What we want so much may not be what we want after all.

16. Who is Right?

Two men were arguing over a certain matter. They both went separately to see the village chief. The village chief told the first man, 'You are right.' He also said to the second man, 'You are right.'

His assistant heard both conversations and asked the village chief, 'Master, they can't both be right.'

The village chief replied, 'You are right, too.'

Lesson: In life, there is no clear-cut right or wrong in several matters. Many arguments can be avoided if we see the other's point of view and accept it as valid as ours.

17. Rainy and Sunny Days

Madam Rani was always sad. One day, a kind, wise neighbour asked her why she was gloomy all the time.

Madam Rani replied, 'I have two daughters — one selling umbrellas to make a living and the other selling cold drinks. When it rains, I think of the daughter selling cold drinks, and when it is sunny, I think of the daughter selling umbrellas.'

The neighbour then advised her, 'Why don't you reverse your thinking? When it rains, think of your daughter selling umbrellas, and when it is sunny, think of your daughter selling cold drinks.'

Madam Rani heeded the neighbour's advice and a smile could be seen on her face.

Lesson: As it is commonly said, 'Change the way you look at things and the things you look at will change.' The way you see things affects how you feel.

18. In the Movie

Jason was watching a movie in a cinema. Halfway through, two ladies in front of him started to chit-chat continuously. As the conversation got louder and seemed non-stop, Jason was very disturbed and could no longer stand it.

He told the ladies, 'Madam, if you don't mind, I can't hear properly.'

One of the ladies retorted, 'This is a private conversation. It is not meant for you to listen.'

Lesson: Do not expect others to see your problems easily.

19. The King and His Assistant (A tale from Ancient India)

There was a king who had a very optimistic assistant. The assistant would see or say something good on anything bad. One day, the king injured his foot while on an outing. The injury was so severe that one of his toes was cut off. The assistant remarked joyfully that it was good. The king was so infuriated that he threw his assistant to jail. A few months later, the king went alone hunting in a deep forest. He was captured by a tribe and brought back to its chief priest as a sacrifice to the gods. The chief priest saw the king had a missing toe. As he was doubtful whether the gods would accept a less than perfect sacrifice, he asked the tribe to release the king. The king pondered over the near-death experience and recalled what his assistant had said when his toe was cut off. He felt remorseful and went to the jail to release his assistant. He apologised to his assistant for putting him in jail. The assistant replied that it too was a good thing. He said, 'If you had not sent me to jail, I would have accompanied you to the forest. And the tribe would offer me as the sacrifice to their gods.'

Lesson: Look for something good in anything bad.

20. Mirror, Mirror on the Wall

Linda, a middle-aged lady, was whining to a friend.

Linda: The other day, I took a look at myself at the mirror. It was very depressing. There is more and more white hair, my face is full of wrinkles, and my arms are flabby …sigh.

Friend: Well, at least your eyesight is still good.

Lesson: There is always something to be thankful for.

21. An Antique Vase

Wang bought a beautiful vase from an antique shop. He liked it very much and would adore and clean it every day. About a month later, an old friend came to visit him. He was excited to show the treasured vase to his friend. He was expecting that his friend would also admire the vase. To his utter disappointment, his friend instead commented, 'What an ugly stuff. It has fallen out of fashion. You should be collecting modern glass ornaments. They are so classy, sparkling and bright.'

Since then, the more Wang looked at his vase the more it looked like an ugly trash his friend said. He finally put it away in a closet and never touched it again. His wife was puzzled how his friend's remarks would cause him to neglect totally a vase he once loved so much.

Lesson 1: We can be easily influenced by others. Learn to be more discriminating when it comes to others' opinions. It is within your power to accept them wholly or partly, or reject them altogether.

Lesson 2: Perception is powerful. The same thing can be viewed differently by different people or differently at different times by the same person.

22. The Sheep and the Pig (Aesop's Fables)

One day, a shepherd caught a young pig. He was carrying the pig to the butcher in the market place. The pig was struggling and squealing at the top of his voice. A sheep said to the pig, 'Why are you kicking up such a fuss? When mister carries us, we don't behave this ridiculously,' The pig replied, 'When mister carries you, he is only after your wool. When he carries me, he is after my life.'

Lesson: Do not judge the behaviour of others. We do not understand fully the situation they are in.

23. Two Salesmen

Salesman 1: Today I made some valuable contacts.

Salesman 2: I didn't get any orders either.

Lesson: The same thing can be said in different ways.

24. My Married Children

Mdm Leong was talking to an old friend about her two married children.

Mdm Leong: My daughter has a wonderful marriage. Her husband always helps her around the house. He will take care of the laundry, wash the dishes, cook most meals, and look after their baby girl.

Friend: How lucky is your daughter.

Mdm Leong: But my son is not so lucky. He is married to an inconsiderate and lazy wife who expects him to take care of the laundry, wash the dishes, cook most meals, and look after their baby boy.

Lesson: The same situation but with opposite viewpoints when seen from different perspectives.

25. A Black Dot

One day a college English teacher handed out the essay test papers to his students. The students were surprised that the paper had only a black dot on it with the instruction 'Write anything you see.'

When the test was over and after going through the papers his students had written, the teacher said to the class, 'Today's exercise is not to test your essay writing. It is to test your thinking, your attitude towards life. All of you have written something on the black dot, but nothing at all on the white paper. The white paper represents our life and the black dot problems in our life. Everyone focused on the black dot and ignored the white paper. This is the same with our lives. We only concentrate on those areas in our life with problems, the black dots. Do not just fill your mind with the black dots. Appreciate the other larger area of the white paper and you will be happier.

Lesson: Life can never be perfect. There are bound to be black dots in our lives. We tend to focus on the few things that are wrong in our lives and forget the far many things that are right. Our happiness depends on where we focus.

Chapter 10

Pleasing Everybody

1. Father, Son and Donkey (Aesop's Fables)

Once, there was a father, son and their donkey travelling from one village to another. Both father and son were riding on the donkey. As they passed by the village, they overheard some villagers commenting that they were so cruel to the poor donkey. So they came down and walked along with the donkey. As they walked, they overheard some villagers commenting that they were so stupid — why not ride on the donkey instead of walking by foot? The son then rode on the donkey. This time, they overheard some villagers commenting that the son was inconsiderate and should have let his old father ride on the donkey. So the father rode on the donkey and the son walked. Soon, they overheard comments that the father was so unkind to his young son for riding on the donkey and letting the child walk. Finally, both father and son carried the donkey as they proceeded.

Lesson: You cannot please everybody. Whatever you do will invite criticisms from some corners.

2. 'Fresh Fish Sold Here'

A fishmonger put up the sign 'Fresh fish sold here' above his stall.

A customer told him to remove *here* as it is redundant. 'It must be here and not elsewhere,' the customer advised. So he erased the word.

Another customer suggested to him to remove the word *sold*. 'It is understood you are selling fish here,' the second customer reasoned. The fishmonger then erased the word.

A third customer advised, 'By saying "fresh", you may arouse suspicion that your fish are not fresh. Customers can see that your fish are fresh.' Again, the fishmonger listened to the advice and erased the word.

Another customer asked, 'Why say "fish"? Everyone knows they are fish.' The fishmonger then erased the last word and brought down the sign.

Two days later, a lady came and, seeing that the sign was removed, asked the fishmonger, 'Why did you remove the sign — "Fresh fish sold here"? I asked my maid to buy fish from the stall with the sign yesterday but she could not find it. So she bought fish from the wrong stall.' On hearing this, the fishmonger wrote the sign and put it up again.

Lesson: You can listen to others' advice, but it is not necessary to follow it. You have to decide for yourself what is good for you.

Chapter 11

Postponement

1. 'Free Lunch Tomorrow'

A popular restaurant in a busy business district had this notice at the entrance: 'Free Lunch Tomorrow'. Every day, a number of officer workers went to the restaurant looking forward to the free lunch but only seeing the same notice and never getting the free lunch.

Lesson 1: Tomorrow never comes.

Lesson 2: We can postpone something to tomorrow indefinitely.

2. A Box of Pears

A man bought a box of pears. Every day, he would pick an overripe, rotten pear and eat. In the end, he ate a box of rotten pears.

Lesson: Life is like that. Do not live such that you end up eating rotten pears your whole life. Do not just focus on the bad things and ignore the good ones. If you pick up things to worry about every day, you live your whole life worrying.

3. When Does Life Begin?

Three men were discussing when life begins.

Man 1: Life begins at the time of conception.

Man 2: Life begins at birth.

Man 3: Life begins when the children are married and all mortgages have been paid.

Lesson: Has life begun in you? If you keep postponing life, you will end up not really living.

4. Changing Diapers

Mary and Leon just had a baby. Mary asked Leon to help change the diapers several times. Every time, Leon would reply, 'I am busy. The next time.' One day, Mary again asked Leon to change the diapers. She said, 'You have said the next time several times.' Leon replied sheepishly, 'I meant the next baby.'

Lesson: We are inclined to keep postponing an unpleasant task indefinitely.

Chapter 12

Pride/Ego

1. <u>A Professor and a Zen Master</u>

Once, an eminent professor went to see a grand master to learn the art of Zen. When he met the master, he kept talking about his knowledge and achievements. The master kept pouring tea on a cup that was already full.

The professor said, 'Master, please stop pouring. The cup is already full.'

The master replied, 'Just like no more tea can go into a cup that is full, I cannot teach you anything if you are already full of knowledge.'

<u>Lesson:</u> To learn something, you have to be humble and empty yourself.

2. **What Is God's Job? (A tale from Ancient India)**

Once, there was a haughty king. Whenever he asked a question, he would demand an answer promptly.

At one time, he asked his prime minister, 'A king rules, a prime minister advises, a teacher teaches, a doctor heals, and a farmer grows vegetables. What is God's job?'

The prime minister was at a loss. He replied, 'I advise you on worldly matters. Since this question concerns the spiritual, I suggest you ask the chief priest.' The king agreed.

The king then asked the chief priest. The chief priest begged for three days to give a reply. The chief priest went to search the scriptures and books for an answer. The third day was approaching, and he still could not find a satisfactory answer to the king's question. He looked sad and worried.

A shepherd boy passed by and asked him why. He explained his problem to the shepherd boy. The shepherd boy asked him not to worry and that he had the answer. But he would like to answer to the king himself.

The chief priest then brought the shepherd boy to the king. The shepherd boy told the king that he had the answer to his question.

The shepherd boy said to the king who was sitting on the throne, 'Since I am answering your question, I am your teacher and you are the student as far as this question is concerned. I therefore request that you come down from your throne and I take your place.'

The king was impressed by the boy's confidence and was also very eager to know the answer. He did as the boy requested and came down sitting on the floor together with the rest present.

There was a moment of silence as the boy was enjoying the court scene from his exalted place.

The king then asked, 'So, what is God's job?'

The boy proclaimed confidently, 'God's job is to push down the haughty and bring up the humble.'

Lesson: Be humble or else you will fall.

3. A Sack of Potatoes

A man went to consult a sage.

Man: Master, I have this problem. I am easily angered, offended, or irritated by people or events. What can I do to get rid of such negative feelings?

The sage gave the man a sack and a basket of potatoes.

Sage: For one week, whenever someone or something bothers you, write the name or matter on a potato, put it inside the sack, and carry the sack wherever you go. Come back to me in a week's time.

In the next meeting one week later, the sage asked, 'Is it a burden to carry the sack around?'

The man replied, 'Definitely it is. Also, as days went by, some potatoes turned bad and started to stink.'

Pride/Ego

The sage continued, 'The potatoes in the sack represent the ill feelings we carry within ourselves. Unless we get rid of them, we will continue to be burdened. Throwing away the potatoes signifies forgiving those who offended us or forgetting things that bothered us. Will you remove the potatoes from the sack and throw them away? Bring the sack back and repeat the exercise for another week.'

The man was eager to throw away the potatoes but reluctant to do the same thing again for another week. He asked, 'Why don't I throw away the sack?'

The sage smiled as the man had learnt the lesson, 'Yes, exactly. The sack represents our inflated self-importance. Not going around collecting potatoes and putting them into the sack is like not allowing people or events to bother us.'

Lesson: The cause of our irritation is our self-importance. As Don Juan taught us, 'Self-importance is man's greatest enemy. Self-importance requires that we spend most of our lives offended by someone.'

4. An Empty Boat (A parable from Chuang Tzu)

A man was boating on a calm river. Suddenly, he saw another boat coming towards him. He shouted at the other boat and tried to avert a collision. But the other boat kept moving forward and collided with his boat. The man was very angry and shouted. He soon realised that it was an empty boat. He stopped shouting and cursing, and his anger subsided.

Lesson: Be like an empty boat. Nobody can insult, harm, or 'be angry with' someone emptied of his/her ego.

5. The Monkey and the Dolphin

Once, there was a group of people who went sailing. One of them brought along his pet monkey. Unfortunately, in the deep sea, they encountered a storm. The small ship capsized. Luckily for the monkey, a dolphin swam along and picked him up. After swimming for a while, the dolphin rested near an island and let the monkey down. The dolphin asked the monkey whether he knew about the island.

The monkey replied, 'My father is the king of this island, and I will soon be the king.'

The dolphin then said, 'You are the king of the island now.'

The monkey wondered and asked, 'How is that so?'

The dolphin replied, 'There is no one staying on this island.', and swam away without the monkey.

Lesson: Nobody likes to help a boastful person.

6. My Genius Boy

A mother was having a conversation with a teacher during a parent-teacher tea session. The mother said proudly of his son, 'I think my son Brian is a genius. He has many original ideas, doesn't he?' The form teacher replied, 'Yes, especially when it comes to spelling.'

Lesson: Do not praise yourself or your loved ones too much.

7. The Ass Carrying a Golden Idol

Pride/Ego

A revered golden idol was to be moved from one temple to another in a town. The temple priest placed the idol on the back of an ass. As the ass passed through the town, the people bowed before the idol.

The ass thought that the people were worshipping him. He thought to himself, 'I am different and important. Why should I work so hard and be exploited by men?' He stopped moving and refused to move an inch when prompted by the guide. As it was near the destination, the guide took the idol down and bring it to the temple. Before that, he gave the ass a good kick.

As the ass went on his way, he found that the people were no longer bowing to him.

Lesson: **Do not take credit that is not due to you, and do not over estimate yourself.**

Chapter 13

Struggles/Adversities

1. Making Tea

A young man was very troubled with his life. He went to consult a Zen master. While the man was pouring out his problems, the Zen master made a cup of tea for him with lukewarm water. He then asked the young man whether he liked the tea. The young man replied that it was tasteless. The Zen master then made a new cup of tea, this time with boiling water. The young man savored the fragrant tea. The Zen master said, 'Life is like tea leaves. Without being subjected to boiling, its best flavour cannot be brought out.'

Lesson: Trying circumstances can bring out the best in a person.

2. The Courage to Live

Amy was beset with problems. She was contemplating suicide. While sitting on her desk, tears flowed and dropped onto the table. She saw an ant struggling to get out of a puddle of her tears. She suddenly realised that if an ant was struggling to be alive, she should have the courage to live.

Lesson: Life is precious. Whatever the problems are, 'This, too, shall pass.'

3. A Lesson in Adversity

One day, a mule fell into a well. The farmer tried all means to rescue it but to no avail. Finally, he decided it could not be saved and asked some of his friends to help throw in sand to bury it and end its misery.

As the sand were shovelled into the well, the mule would shake them off and stood above them. Soon, the sand was raised to a level where the mule could get off the well triumphantly.

Lesson: When life throws problems at us, we have the choice to let them bury us or shake them off and rise above them.

4. Obstacles

A king asked his men to place a big rock in the middle of a road. Everyone passing by the road just walked around the rock without bothering to move it to the side for the convenience of others. Several just cursed the person who put the rock there and moved on. One farmer with a load of vegetables came. He put down his stuff and, with all his strength, moved the rock to the side. He saw an envelope lying below the big rock. He picked it up. To his pleasant surprise, it was a reward of a few gold pieces from the king for the person who removed the rock.

Lesson: **An obstacle may pave the way for something good.**

5. A Teaspoon of Salt

An unhappy young man went to see a counsellor. He was sharing with the counsellor his bitterness in life. The counsellor put a teaspoon of salt into a small cup of water and asked the man to drink it. 'The taste was unbearable, right?' asked the counsellor. The counsellor then put another teaspoon of salt into a large jug of water. This time the water was drinkable.

The counsellor then explained, 'The pain in life is like a teaspoon of salt. The amount of pain is the same, but the degree of bitterness depends on the size of the container. To reduce your sufferings in life, enlarge your sense of being. Stop being a small cup; be a large jug.'

Lesson: **One way to manage your problems in life is to widen your horizon. Do not just have a narrow focus on yourself.**

6. Carrot, Egg and Tea Leaves

A master was teaching a small group of disciples on how an adversity could affect different people differently. He prepared three identical pots and filled them with the same amount of water. He then boiled a carrot, an egg and some tea leaves separately in each pot.

He then said, 'Each item is subjected to the same circumstances but it turned out differently. The carrot became soft. The egg became hard. The tea leaves turned the water into a pot of aromatic tea.'

The master explained further, 'When faced with an adversity, do not be like the carrot which turns soft or the egg which turns hard.

Rather, be like the tea leaves which bring forth their best essence and change the circumstances for the better.'

Lesson: How we respond to an adversity can turn it into something positive or negative.

7. The Butterfly Story

A young man, strolling in a garden, saw a cocoon opening up. He stood there for quite a while, but the butterfly was still struggling to get out of the tight cocoon. Ignorant that the struggle was nature's way of giving the emerging butterfly a strong wing, he thought he should help the butterfly by cutting open the cocoon.

With a wide opening, the butterfly came out of the cocoon. However, it could not soar high for the rest of its life because of the kind but misdirected act of the young man.

Lesson: Struggles are part and parcel of life. If we go through life without any obstacles, it might inhibit our growth. We would not be as strong as we could have been.

8. One Hundred Camels

A young man beset by a host of problems went to seek counsel from a wise master. He asked the master how he could solve all his problems so that he could start to live a peaceful and happy life. The master replied, 'I will let you know tomorrow. But first you help me to look after my hundred camels tonight as the caretaker is sick. You must not sleep unless all the camels sit or lie down to have a proper rest.'

The next day, the master met the young man who apparently did not sleep the whole night.

Master: You didn't sleep the whole night?

Young Man: I could not sleep at all because there was not a single moment where all the camels sat down. When I managed to get one to sit down, few others would stand up. Some refused to sit down even after much prodding. Some sat down on their own.

Master: Isn't what you experienced last night the same with our problems in life? At any stage of our life, there are problems. Some will be resolved by themselves. Some you can solve, but new ones will appear. Some cannot be resolved even with your effort. Just like you could not sleep last night because you waited until all the camels sat down, you will not start to live a peaceful and happy life if you wait until all your problems are resolved. Problems are part of life.

Lesson: It is futile to wait until you have no problems to start living a peaceful and happy life.

Chapter 14

Miscellaneous: Other Life Truths

1. A Woodcutter

Once, there was a woodcutter toiling hard in a wood. He saw a rich, powerful man being carried comfortably on a sedan chair. He said to himself, 'I want to be a rich, powerful man.' So he became a rich, powerful man. While being carried on a sedan chair, the blazing sun shone on his face. He said to himself, 'I want to be a sun.' So he became a sun. A cloud passed by and blocked him. He said to himself, 'I want to be a cloud.' So he became a cloud. Soon, wind blew him away. He said to himself, 'I want to be a wind.' So he became a wind. He could blow away many things, but the trees seemed to be stronger than he. He said to himself, 'I want to be a tree.' So he became a tree. One day, he heard chopping sound. There he saw a woodcutter cutting down trees. He said to himself, 'I want to be a woodcutter.' So he became a woodcutter, back to where he originally was.

Lesson: **There is always someone/something else superior to another one/another thing. Anyone/anything is superior in his/its own way.**

2. The Deer and His Antlers (Aesop's Fables)

Once, there was a deer who admired his antlers very much. He would spend much time looking at his antlers over a lake. On the other hand, he was ashamed of his legs and hated to look at them as he felt that they were skinny and awful. One day, he was chased by a lion. His legs took him as far as they could. Just as he was beginning to feel relieved as the lion was some distance away, his antlers got stuck by a tree branch. The lion soon caught up with him.

Lesson: **A thing which looks beautiful may be useless or even harmful. A thing which seems dull may turn out to be of practical value.**

3. Two Wishes

Two men, Keith and Andrew, were stranded on an island. One day, a genie appeared and offered each of them two wishes.

Keith clamoured to say first. He stated his two wishes, 'Send me home and make me a millionaire.' His wishes were granted.

When it was Andrew's turn, he said, 'Send me home and bring Keith back.' His wishes were also granted.

Lesson: First is not necessarily the best. Do not always fight to be the first. Be more gracious and let others go first.

4. What Is Intelligence?

Two men, John and Matthew, were working in a cave. John asked Matthew why they had to slog hard in the cave while their boss sat comfortably in an air-conditioned room. Matthew suggested John to ask their boss. John went to ask the boss. The boss replied that it was because he had intelligence.

'What is it?' John asked.

The boss said, 'I'll put my hand on the wall and you hit it.'

When John was about to hit hard his boss's hand, his boss quickly moved his hand away and John hit the wall. John understood the meaning of intelligence and returned to the cave. Matthew asked him what the boss had said.

John replied, 'He said that it is because he has intelligence.'

'What is it?' Matthew asked.

Looking for a wall in the cave but not finding any, John said, 'I'll put my hand on my face and you hit it.'

Lesson: A response that is correct or suitable in one situation may not be so in another.

5. A Large Pizza

A man ordered a large pizza for himself in a fast-food restaurant. The waitress asked whether she should cut it into six or twelve pieces. The man replied, 'Six pieces, please. I cannot finish eating twelve pieces.'

Lesson: **It is easy to deceive ourselves.**

6. Do Not Accept the Gift

Once, Buddha was teaching a group of disciples. A man kept abusing him verbally. However, Buddha remained calm and was not in any way affected. One disciple asked Buddha how he could ignore the verbal abuses.

Buddha asked him, 'If someone gives you a gift and you do not accept it, does the gift belong to you?'

The man answered, 'No, it is still with the giver.'

'It is the same with someone giving you abuses,' replied Buddha.

Lesson: **When someone abuses or insults you, you do not have to take it personally. You can simply ignore it. Richard Carlson in his book** ***Don't Sweat the Small Stuff and It's All Small Stuff*** **taught us a similar lesson — 'If someone throws you a ball, you don't have to catch it.'**

7. An English Professor

An English professor wrote this on a student's examination script: 'Never begin a sentence with *and* or end one with a preposition. This is an important grammatical rule observed by good writers. And it is a practice all students should stick to.'

Lesson: Practise what you preach.

{Note: This story is just to illustrate a lesson. It does not indicate a belief in such a grammatical rule.}

8. Hidden Treasures

One day, God wanted to hide some treasures from men. He consulted a wise angel. 'Shall I hide them in the moon?' God asked.

The angel replied, 'No, men will find a way to reach the moon.'

'What about the highest mountain or the deepest ocean?' God asked.

The angel again replied, 'No, men will scale the highest mountain and dive into the deepest ocean.'

The angel then said, 'Hide them in the heart of men. They will never find them.'

Lesson: What you are seeking could well be very near you. As Emerson put it, 'God hides things by putting them near us.' As someone also said, 'The truth you seek is not hidden from you. You are hiding from it.'

9. The Cracked Bucket

Fatima would fetch water from a well every morning with two buckets. One of the buckets had a crack on its base. When Fatima reached home, the cracked bucket would contain less than half of the water collected. The good bucket had been looking down on the cracked bucket. One day, the good bucket said to the cracked bucket, 'You are so useless. While I brought back the water full, you only carried less than half.' The cracked bucket was very sad.

The next morning, the cracked bucket was sobbing when Fatima was about to go for her daily round of collecting water. Upon knowing the reason for its sadness, Fatima said to the cracked bucket, 'Do you see the beautiful flowers along the way back from the well? I watered them with the water leaked from you. Your effort is not wasted.' Upon hearing that, the cracked bucket was happy that it was not that useless as the good bucket thought so.

Lesson: As a Chinese saying goes, 'Whatever heaven bestows on me, they must be of some use.' Everybody has different abilities, but everyone can contribute.

10. Four Frogs on a Log

Father: There were four frogs on a log. Three decided to jump off. How many frogs were left on the log?

Son: One.

Father: Wrong.

Son: Why?

Father: The three frogs that decided to jump did not eventually jump.

Lesson: There is a world of difference between deciding and doing. Intention is not the same as action.

11. A Dog's Tail

Father: How many legs does a dog have if we called its tail a leg?

Son: Five.

Father: Wrong.

Son: Why?

Father: Calling a tail a leg does not make it so.

Lesson: Facts are facts and we cannot change them.

12. Counting beyond 10

A nursery teacher asked her class whether anyone knew how to count beyond 10. Little Johnny put up his hand, stood up and proudly recited, '1, 2, 3, 4, 5, 6, 7, 8, 9, 10, J, Q, K.'

Lesson: We never know what children learnt from adults.

13. Flight Delay

The plane finally took off after a two-hour delay. One passenger asked the chief flight attendant what the cause of the delay was. She replied, 'The first pilot heard some noise from the engines and was worried. We managed to find another pilot who was not concerned about the engine noise.'

Lesson: A problem is not solved until the root cause is tackled.

14. The Starfish Story

In a beach, there were several stray starfish swept ashore. An old man was picking up the starfish and threw them back to the sea one by one. A young man asked him why he was doing so. The old man replied that he was saving the starfish as they could not survive on the shore under the hot sun.

The young man asked, 'But there are so many beaches with starfish along the shore. You are wasting your time and energy. What difference can you make?'

The old man replied as he was throwing one starfish back to the sea, 'I am making a difference to this one.'

Lesson: **Just because we cannot do everything does not mean we cannot do anything. Or as Saint Theresa said, 'If we cannot feed a hundred, just feed one.' If everyone does his/her part in making a difference, the world will be a better place.**

15. A Chessboard and a Grain of Rice (A Persian tale)

One day, a man presented a chessboard to the king. The king was so impressed with the gift and he offered to reward the man. The king asked the man what he would like to have. The man replied that he would want a grain of rice on the first box of the chessboard and double the quantity for every subsequent box (there are sixty-four squares in a chessboard). The king was surprised at the seemingly modest request and agreed immediately. It was when the palace tried to fulfil the man's request that they realised it could not be met.

Lesson: **Be aware of the power of exponential growth. Try this: Which is more — I give you $1,000 a day for thirty days or (B) I give you 1 cent and double it every day for thirty days, that is, 1 cent on the first day and 2 cents the second day and so on?**

{Get ready your Excel worksheet. For (A) you get $30,000. For (B) you get more than $10 million!}

16. <u>Skills or Luck</u>

Robert was very successful in stock and other financial tradings. One day, he was having a conversation with his old friend, Albert. Albert opined that luck was the main reason for Robert's success in making lots of money. Robert maintained that his skills were the main contributing factors for his success. They argued for a while until Albert finally retorted, 'You must agree that you are lucky to have the skills.'

<u>Lesson:</u> Luck does play a significant part in our lives. Life is like a game of cards. Some are given fortuitous cards. Others are given less favourable cards. We cannot control the cards given to us, but we can control how we play out the game.

17. <u>Empty Promises</u>

Boy: If you have two houses, would you give me one?

Girl: Yes, I will.

Boy: If you have two cars, would you give me one?

Girl: Definitely.

Boy: If you have two chocolate bars, would you give me one?

Girl (crying): That is not fair. You know I have two chocolate bars.

<u>Lesson:</u> Empty promises are easy to make.

18. The Navy

Johnny had been very keen to join the navy since he was young. Whenever there was a navy open house, his parents would bring him there and he would spend hours on board a navy ship. One day, Johnny realised his dream and joined the navy. But he didn't seem happy. His aunt asked him why.

Johnny replied, 'I used to be very interested in the navy as I was very impressed by a navy ship. Its orderliness and the equipment on board are spotless. Now I know who keep them in such a speck-free condition.'

Lesson: We are here not to partake in the good things without playing our part.

19. No Choice

It was mealtime on a flight. An attendant asked a passenger, 'Would you like to have dinner?'

The passenger answered, 'What are my choices?'

The flight attendant replied, 'Yes or no.'

Lesson: In life, you have to accept that sometimes you are not given much choice.

20. Fire Exit

Bar owner to a customer: You cannot stand here. You are blocking the fire exit.

Customer: Don't worry, boss. I won't be standing here if there is a fire.

Lesson: Understand the intention behind a rule. It is not always necessary to follow rules rigidly.

21. Sun or Moon

Two men were arguing which was more important — the sun or the moon. One of them said that the moon was more important. He reasoned, 'The moon shines in the dark where we need the light, whereas the sun shines during the day where there is already plenty of light.'

Lesson: It is easy to take things for granted and forget the source of goodness.

22. Statistics

A defence agency of a certain country kept statistics on the number of road accidents involving their vehicles. The commanders were concerned over the high number of such accidents. One smart alec suggested to change the definition of accidents to include only those where their soldier drivers were at fault. Otherwise, the case would be classified as an 'incident' instead of an 'accident'. After such a change, the statistics on the number of accidents remained much the same.

Lesson: We cannot hide the truth.

23. Wrong Number

Joe's wife could talk for hours over the phone. Once, she put down the phone after only about fifteen minutes. Joe was surprised and asked her whom she had talked to. She replied, 'She called the wrong number.'

Lesson: It is difficult to change human nature.

24. The Toddler Who Tried to Catch His Shadow

A toddler was playing in a garden one evening. He saw his shadow and was trying to catch hold of his head in the shadow. He ran fast with his hand stretched but could not reach it. Frustrated, he stopped and cried. A passer-by who was watching him came and consoled him and told him to touch his head. At last, the toddler got what he wanted.

Lesson: What you are looking for may not be outside you but is inside or near you.

25. A Miser

Tony was in a gift shop buying a birthday present for his girlfriend. The sales assistant showed him a bottle of perfume. Tony shook his head and commented that it was too expensive. The sales assistant then brought him a smaller bottle. Again, Tony shook his head. She then suggested a set of cosmetic jewelleries. Again, Tony did not want and asked, 'Can I see something cheap?' The sales assistant handed over a small mirror to him.

Lesson: You do not have to be extravagant. But also do not be a miser.

26. Monster Melons (A Sufi story)

Once, there was a man who strayed into a remote island. The people in the island were strange. They had a weird fear of watermelons which was passed down from generations. They thought that watermelons were evil monsters. The man cut a watermelon and ate it. He was satisfied that he had dispelled once and for all the queer fear of the islanders. However, it was not quite so. The islanders became more fearful of him than of the watermelons. They thought that he was a worse monster and that he would next kill them one by one. One day, they drove the man away from the island.

Soon, another man strayed into the island. Unlike the first man, he did not immediately quash the islander's deep-seated fear of watermelons. Instead, he behaved like the islanders in fearing the watermelons. Slowly, he won their trust. Then he showed them that watermelons were just juicy fruits. He even taught the islanders how to plant more watermelons.

Lesson: You cannot change a person overnight. You need to win his trust first.

27. The Monastery's Cat

In a monastery in old Tibet, the monks practised tying up the monastery's cat to a tree before the start of a meditation session and untying it after that. This was carried out as instructed by the founding chief monk so as not to let the cat distract the monks in meditation. It had become part of the daily ritual. One day, the cat died. The monks were at a loss as to what to do. They then decided to look for a new cat to continue the practice.

Lesson: Do not follow a practice blindly. Understand the reason behind it.

28. Rocks, Pebbles and Sand

One day, a philosophy professor gave a demonstration before a small class. He asked one of the students to put some rocks in a jar. After that, he asked the student to put some pebbles, then sand into the jar. The jar was filled with rocks, pebbles and sand. Next, the professor asked another student to fill the jar in the reverse order — sand, pebbles and rocks. After putting in the sand and pebbles, not all the rocks could go into the jar.

The professor then explained the purpose of the demonstration. He said, 'Look at the rocks as the most important things in your life — your health, well-being, safety and family. The pebbles are like those things that matter but not that really important — money and other material things above what are essential. The sand represents the unimportant, small stuff. If you attend to the unimportant or less important things first, you have no time for the really important matters.'

Lesson: Take care of the important things in life first. The less important things will follow. Prioritise.

29. A Child Psychologist and an Elderly Lady

Once, a young man and an elderly lady were seated together on a flight. A conversation soon struck up. The lady said that she was heading home after spending two weeks with her three children, five grandchildren and a great-grandchild living in the same city. She then asked the young man what he did for a living. The man introduced himself as a child psychologist and said that he was flying to attend a seminar on child development and discipline. He was eagerly waiting to offer free advice to the lady. Instead, the elderly lady asked, 'Well, if there is anything you like to know, feel free to ask me.'

Lesson: Practical knowledge is more important than theories.

30. Answered with a Question

Boss: Why is it that whenever I asked you something, you would answer with another question?

Worker: Oh, was it what I did?

Lesson: Habits die hard.

31. Test for Sanity

A reporter visited a mental hospital and interviewed its director, who was also a renowned psychiatrist.

The reporter asked, 'How will you determine whether a patient needs to stay in the hospital?'

The director replied, 'I will fill a bathtub to the full and give the patient a scoop, a mug and a bucket and ask him to empty the bathtub.'

The reporter interjected, 'A normal person would use the bucket.'

The director retorted, 'A normal person would unplug the bathtub.'

Lesson: Beware of things that make something obvious less so. In this story, if the patient is not given a scoop, mug and bucket, the solution may be more obvious.

32. How Many Biscuits Can You Eat on an Empty Stomach?

John: How many biscuits can you eat on an empty stomach?

Tom: One hundred.

John: Wrong. After you have eaten one biscuit, your stomach is no longer empty.

Tom was impressed with the joke. He was eager to play it on his wife that evening.

Tom: How many biscuits can you eat on an empty stomach?

Tom's wife: I think fifty.

Tom, visibly disappointed, said, 'If you had told me one hundred, I would be able to share a good joke with you.'

Lesson: Be flexible.

33. Forever Grateful

Lester: Last year, I was in need of money and you gave me. I said I would not forget your kindness.

Jimmy: I remember.

Lester: Well, I am broke again.

Lesson: If you help someone in need, he is sure to remember you — the next time he needs your help.

34. The Fox Who Lost His Tail (Aesop's Fables)

Once, there was a fox who had his tail accidentally cut off while escaping from a trap. Although the fox was much relieved to have escaped, he soon became sad and embarrassed to find his tail gone. The fox called a meeting with all other foxes. He tried to persuade the rest to cut off their tail, saying that the tail was useless and a hindrance when sitting, and that it would make it easier for chasing wild dogs to catch. All the foxes were not convinced and walked away. The fox was disappointed and walked away sadly.

Lesson: Beware of someone who would dread you down to suffer his woes with him.

35. Parking

Roger was frantically looking for a parking lot in a building as he had an important appointment. As there was no parking lot in sight and there were few cars waiting to park, he started to utter a prayer earnestly, 'God, please find me a parking lot. I'll go to church every week and pray every day.' Soon after, he saw a car moving out of a parking lot near him and he said, 'Oh, never mind, God. I found one.'

Lesson: Some people are often ungrateful and can easily forget the help extended to them.

36. Spelling

Teacher: Johnny, how do you spell crocodile?

Little Johnny: K-R-O-K-O-D-I-L-E.

Teacher: That is wrong, Johnny.

Little Johnny: It can't be. You asked me how I spell it.

Miscellaneous: Other Life Truths

Lesson: What you think is right may not be necessarily so.

37. Learning a Lesson

Things were not going fine in a highly regimented army camp. Rumours were circulating, and the morale of the men was low. One private soldier was caught for gossiping. He was charged and duly sentenced to death. On the day of the 'execution', he was shot but did not die.

The general then said to him sternly, 'We had just fired a blank to scare you. Do not spread rumours again or you will face the real punishment. Hope you have learnt a lesson. You can go now.'

The soldier ran back to his bunk. Upon seeing his bunk mates, he said, 'You know something? Our camp does not have live ammunitions.'

Lesson: Some people will never learn a lesson.

38. How a Centipede Walks

One day, a centipede was stopped by a knowledgeable and analytical frog who said, 'I have been observing how you walk. I just wondered how you manage to coordinate your movements with 100 legs. How do you know which legs to move?'

The centipede was puzzled as he had not considered such a question before. From that day onwards, he had difficulties walking as he kept thinking how to move his legs.

Lesson: If you are too self-conscious of what you are doing, you will have difficulties getting things done.

39. Name Calling

Clever Jenny: This is such an easy sum and you couldn't solve. You are so stupid.

Hurtful Joe: I feel insulted when you called me stupid. I have never called you short and fat and ugly!

Lesson: Sometimes we do the very things we say we are not doing.

40. The Navy Officer and His Men

One night, a navy captain fell off while alone on the deck. A private saw the incident and quickly jumped into the sea and rescued the captain. The captain, saved and shocked, was of course very grateful to the private. He said, 'Private Martin, words cannot express my gratitude to you for saving my life. I will tell all men your courageous act and richly reward you, including a promotion.'

The private, expressing concern, replied, 'Sir, please do not do that. The best reward you can give me is to keep quiet about the whole thing. If the men knew that I saved you, they would dump me into the sea.'

Lesson: Sometimes we get to know the truth indirectly.

41. An Obvious Answer

Terry was having a conversation with a psychiatrist friend.

Terry: Is there a simple way you can determine whether a person is mentally normal or not?

Psychiatrist: Yes, I'll ask a very easy question which any normal person will definitely be able to answer.

Terry: Such as?

Psychiatrist: Captain Cook made three trips round the world. He died during one of the trips. Which one?

Terry thought for a moment and, with a tinge of embarrassment, asked, 'Would you have another example? I do not know much about history or adventure.'

Lesson: **Some people just cannot see the obvious, no matter how obvious it is.**

42. A One-Horse Race

Jimmy was a compulsive gambler. One day, he learnt that there was going to be a horse-racing with only one horse taking part. He bet his whole life's savings and also whatever he could sell, including his house.

On the day of the peculiar horse-racing, Jimmy was eagerly waiting to be rich. Alas, the horse ran over the fence halfway and escaped.

Lesson: **Not everything that seems absolutely certain is 100% sure.**

43. A Birthday Wish

Little Joseph was praying very loudly for a bicycle for his coming birthday.

Joseph: Oh, God, please give me a bicycle for my birthday next month!

Mummy: You don't have to pray that loud. God is not deaf.

Joseph: God is not deaf. But granny is hard of hearing.

Lesson: You can pray to God for help, but you also need to do what is within your control.

44. Three Prisoners

Three men were convicted of a crime and sentenced to ten years' jail in a solitary confinement. They were each given a wish to bring something into their cells. Prisoner A asked for as many books as possible and a dictionary. Prisoner B requested painting supplies and a few pieces of fine art. Prisoner C wanted ten years' supply of cigarettes.

What happened to the prisoners at the end of the sentence?

Prisoner A was ready to enrol in a university to further his studies. Prisoner B was looking forward to be an accomplished artist. Well, as for prisoner C, he wasted ten years of his life. He did not even get a puff of cigarette because he forgot to ask for some lighters.

Lesson: What we will be tomorrow depends on what we do today.

45. An Unnecessary Question

Wallace was a door-to-door salesman selling some lady stuff. One day, he knocked at a door. A small kid opened the door. He was carrying a cigarette on one hand and a can of beer in the other, acting like an adult.

Wallace: Is your mom home?

Small kid, taking a sip of beer: 'What do you think?'

Lesson: Do not ask unnecessary questions.

46. Fighting over Nothing (A tale from Ancient China)

Two warriors were strolling in the woods. They met each other and exchanged greetings. Soon they noticed a glaring reflection from nearby. It came from two shining shields — one golden and one silver. They knew the shields were valuable.

Warrior A: I will take the gold one and you take the silver as I saw them first.

Warrior B: I saw them first, or at least we saw them at the same time. I will take the gold one as I am holding a higher rank than you.

Warrior A: Nonsense. I will take the gold one as these woods belong to my lord.

They argued to and fro. And both ran towards the prized shields. Nearing the shields, they took out their swords and fought. As they came closer to the shields, they noticed that both were identical. One with gold on the surface and silver beneath, and the other with silver on the surface and gold beneath.

Both warriors kept their swords, and each took a shield and continued their walk.

Lesson: Are we also fighting and competing over nothing? At the end of it all, we all will get the same thing.

47. A Comic Book

Adrian was caught reading a comic book in class. The teacher snatched it away and said, 'I will return it to you at the end of the term.'

Adrian replied, 'But why? You don't need that long to read it.'

Lesson: Some people are not aware of what is happening around them.

48. Hindsight

An angel appeared during a college faculty meeting. She offered the dean a wish for his dedicated service and exemplary conduct. The dean was given two choices — infinite wisdom or infinite wealth. Without hesitation, the dean chose infinite wisdom. 'Granted,' said the angel, and she departed.

The dean's face was sparkling bright. There was a long silence. One staff member asked, 'Professor Brown, what are you thinking?'

The dean replied, 'I should have taken the money.'

Lesson: Wisdom often comes after we need it.

49. Two Frogs in a Pit

Once, a group of frogs were walking through a wood. Two frogs fell into a deep pit. The other frogs gathered around the pit and lamented the hopeless situation. They shouted at the fallen frogs that it was hopeless to try to get out as the pit was too deep. However, the two frogs tried. After a while, one of them gave up. The other frog continued to jump and kept trying. At last, this frog leaped out of the deep pit. He thanked his friends for cheering and encouraging him. This frog was actually deaf.

Lesson: Do not listen to the negative words of others. What you think you can do, you should proceed.

50. A Cup of Coffee

A group of friends went to visit their former professor. During the conversion, they each lamented how stressful life was. The professor then went to the kitchen and brought a pot of coffee and a tray containing various types of cups — fanciful, exquisite, porcelain, and the plain ones. He noted that the plain cups were left behind.

The professor then tried to teach his former students a lesson in life. He said, 'The cause of all your stress is you are looking for external things, whereas the real thing is the coffee. The coffee represents your life, and the cup are the external things like your car, house, wealth and job. The cup does not define the quality of the coffee. We should not let the type of cup affect our enjoyment of the coffee.'

Lesson: You can enjoy coffee with a fanciful cup or a plain one. Likewise, you can enjoy life without the external trappings.

51. Name on the Door

A philosopher had an appointment to debate with a cheerful village elder. On the appointed time, he went to the elder's house. But the elder was not in. He was playing with the children and telling them stories elsewhere. The philosopher waited for an hour and was very angry. He wrote 'Stupid Fool' on the door of the elder's house and left.

Upon his return, the elder quickly rushed to the philosopher's house. He said, 'I am sorry. I forgot our appointment until I saw your name on the door.'

Lesson: When you throw an insult at others, it could be thrown back at you.

52. Buried Treasures

An old farmer was worried about the livelihood of his three lazy sons after he died. On his deathbed, he told his sons that he had buried a pot of gold in the farm. The sons were listening intensely on where the pot of gold was buried, but the old father passed away.

After that, the sons diligently dug the ground. They could not find any pot of gold. Since the ground was well dug, they thought they might as well plant some crops as their father did. The crops grew well, and they had a harvest. They continued to dig the ground, searching for the pot of gold. Years passed. The sons dug the ground but could not find the pot of gold. They planted crops and had a good harvest. With the harvest from the crops over the years, they managed to live quite happily. They then realised what their father meant by a 'pot of gold' under the ground.

Lesson: To find your pot of gold, you need to put in effort.

53. Three Tortoises Went Picnicking

Once, there were three tortoises who went for a picnic. They brought along a box of sandwiches and cakes, some canned food, and bottles of drinks. They walked for half a day and reached a beautiful beach and settled down. And goodness, they had forgotten to bring along a can opener and a bottle opener. The two elder tortoises persuaded the youngest tortoise to go back and bring the openers. The youngest tortoise was reluctant to go as he feared that his older brothers would eat all the sandwiches and cakes. Finally, he agreed on the assurance that they would wait for him to be back before eating them.

They waited. One day passed. Another day passed by. On the fourth day, the elder tortoises decided to break their promise and open the box of sandwiches and cakes rather than let them spoil. Just then, the youngest tortoise ran out from behind the bush and cried, 'I know you all will eat the sandwiches and cakes and not wait for me!'

Lesson: Sometimes our actions tend towards a self-fulfilling prophecy.

54. 'No, Sir'

Officer (holding a $10 note): Soldier, do you have a small change for $10?

Soldier: Sure, buddy.

Officer: Is that the way you address an officer? Let's do it again. Soldier, do you have a small change for $10?

Soldier: No, Sir!

Lesson: If you insist on formality all the time, you may not get what you want, especially when you are asking for a favour.

55. The Customer Is Always Right

Tom reported for work on the first day as a salesman in an electrical appliance shop. The sales manager gave him a briefing and kept emphasising that 'the customer is always right'. Tom proceeded to work. The manager observed that a customer had a short conversation with Tom and walked away without buying anything. He noted the same thing happened to a few other customers. During lunchtime, the manager asked Tom what happened. Tom replied, 'Those customers commented that our prices were high and I said they were right.'

Lesson: We need to use our discretions at times.

56. A Duel without End (or Rather with a Happy Ending)

Once, there were two neighbouring kingdoms that were always at war over the common border. The kings from both sides decided not to expend so much resources in fighting and agreed to send the best warrior of each kingdom for a duel. On the appointed day, both champion warriors fought in front of a large gathering. They fought from morning till evening and still there was no winner.

Warrior A started to talk, 'When I am fighting you, I am thinking of my wife who is so devastated that our only son was killed by your army.'

Warrior B replied, 'Both my mother and wife were killed by you. These two women were dearest to me. My wife and I grew up together.'

As the conversation continued, they found out each other's family background and story. Soon, they could no longer fight further. It was almost late in the night. They both put down their weapons and shields and embraced each other.

Both kings, who were there, also saw the futility of fighting and agreed to live in peace thereafter.

Lesson: Longfellow said, 'If we could read the secret history of our enemies, we should find in each man's life sorrow and suffering enough to disarm all hostility.' Understanding others' sorrows and struggles in life will help us not to make things difficult for each other.

57. Illegible Handwriting

Student: Teacher, I could not quite make up what you wrote at the margin on my test paper.

Teacher: I told you to write legibly.

Lesson: The fault you see in others is your own fault.

58. Examples

A man saw a fox which had lost a leg. The man wondered how the fox could survive. He then saw a tiger approaching with a big piece of meat. The tiger shared the meat with the fox. That happened every day. The man thought to himself, 'If God can provide for the fox, surely he can provide for me.' He laid back, did nothing and expected to be fed. A few days passed and nothing happened. He was almost starved to death. Then he had a dream and a voice spoke to him, 'You are on the wrong path. You should follow the example of the hardworking, helpful tiger and not the unfortunate, disabled fox.'

Lesson: Choose the right examples to follow.

59. My Ex-Employer

The boss was talking to Mark, a new employee, finding out from him how his work was and what he felt about the company.

Mark replied, 'The work is OK. It is more or less similar to my previous job. But I had far better benefits from my former company. I had free medical coverage for my family and myself, free insurance cover, transport subsidy, meal allowance, and a guaranteed two-month bonus.'

The bemused boss asked, 'Then why did you leave?'

Mark replied sheepishly, 'My former boss went bust.'

Lesson: Nothing too good can last forever.

60. Two Monks Crossing a River

Once, there were two monks about to cross a river. They noticed a young lady who also wanted to cross over. But she appeared hesitant and apprehensive even though the water level was below the knee level. The elder monk then carried her over.

After reaching the bank and walking along, the elder monk noticed that the younger monk was grouchy. He asked the younger monk why.

The younger monk replied, 'Why do you touch the young lady when our vow of chastity forbids us to do so?'

The elder monk replied, 'When I left her at the bank, I have also put her away from my mind. Why are you still carrying her in your mind?'

Lesson: Do not carry unnecessary burden in your mind. Let go.

61. The Angry Nails

Ken was a hot-tempered child. One day, his father thought of a plan to give Ken a lesson on the undesirable consequences of being angry. He would drive a nail onto the wall in Ken's room whenever Ken lost his cool for one month. His father was pleased that over the days, the number of nails was getting fewer.

At the end of the month, Ken's father removed the nails on the wall and told his son, 'Ken, removing the nails is like making amends on those deeds done and words said in anger. You can remove the nails but the holes remain. Likewise, you can make amends, but the scars are difficult or sometimes not possible to remove.'

Lesson: This story illustrates the often said 'Sorry no cure'. These three words are not pleasant to the ears but they are often true.

62. The Fox and the Cat

Mr Fox was well known for his cleverness. One day, a humble cat met the fox. The cat, wanting to learn something from the fox, greeted him with respect.

Cat: Mr Fox, how are you? I heard that you know a lot of things. Can you teach me some?

The fox, full of pride, said, 'Yes, I know a lot of things and have lots of tricks in my sack. What do you know?'

Cat: I know how to catch mice and run very fast and leap when chased by a dog.

Just then, a hunter came with four wild hounds chasing after them. The cat ran very fast and leapt up a tree. The hounds were closing in on the fox. The cat, safe on a low branch, shouted to the fox, 'Mr Fox, quickly take out some tricks from your sack!' Soon the four hounds caught up with the fox. There was no way for the fox to escape.

Lesson: **It is not what you know but how useful the things you know that counts.**

63. The Dog and the Ass (Aesop's Fables)

A man had a pet dog and an ass. The dog was the man's favourite. He liked to play with the dog on his lap. The dog was allowed to run freely in the house. On the other hand, the ass was not allowed into the house. He stayed in a stable outside and had to do all the 'donkey' work all day long. He was envious of the dog's easy life and how the dog could delight their master. One day, the ass decided to be like the dog. He galloped into the house while the master was having his dinner. He tried to leap on the master's lap but hit the dining table, causing the master to almost fall off. The servants quickly shoved the clumsy ass out and gave him a good beating.

Lesson: **Do not imitate others. Be yourself.**

64. The Travellers and the Tree (Aesop's Fables)

Two travellers were resting below a tree with a big shade after a long walk on a hot summer day. One of them said to the other, 'What a useless tree. It does not bear fruits, and the trunk is so crooked and rough. No one can make use of this tree.'

The tree thought, 'I am shielding you from the hot sun and you are resting comfortably here, and yet you deride me for being good-for-nothing. What an ungrateful creature you are.'

Lesson: **It is easy to be ungrateful.**

65. A Cow Farm

Joe owned a cow farm. For many years, he would milk his cows daily. One day, his MBA son figured out that if the cows were to be milked once a week, they would give seven days' worth of milk each time. He worked out a grand productivity plan to roster the cows to be milked weekly. Old Joe, who should know better, listened to his son.

The plan turned out to be devastating. The cows could not give as much milk as before. Several of them also fell sick.

Lesson: The more you give, the more you will have to give. For certain things, as long as you give, the supply will continue. Once you hoard, the supply will stop.

66. Three Monkeys in a Room

John: You are in a room with three monkeys. One is holding a stick, one holding a banana and the third one holding a book. Who is the smartest in the room?

Alex: The one holding a book.

John: I thought it should be you.

Lesson: Our mind tends to be swayed by unimportant, irrelevant details that seem significant.

67. A Woodcutter and His Axe (Aesop's Fables)

A woodcutter was looking for a piece of wood to replace the damaged handle of his axe. He asked the father tree to give him just a small branch. The father tree acceded to his request. As soon as he had a piece of wood, the woodcutter fitted it onto the blade and started to use his axe to chop down several trees. The father tree regretted to have given the woodcutter a small branch.

Lesson: What you have given in a bit may cause you total destruction.

68. The Palace and the Hut

There was a king who wanted a palace on top of a beautiful mountain. When the palace was built, he came to inspect it. He saw an ugly hut next to the grand palace. His men explained that the hut belonged to an old lady who refused to let them demolish it, even when offered a large sum of money. The old lady told the king's officials that the hut was very dear to her as she had spent long memorable years with her husband, who had passed away not too long ago.

The king's men expected that the king would order the hut to be demolished. To their relief and surprise, the king declared, 'Let the hut be there. It will remind me that there are things that money cannot buy.'

Lesson: There are indeed things that money cannot buy.

69. Obey Rules

A boy asked his father when he would be old enough to be freed from all rules he had to obey. The father replied, 'I do not know. I have not come across such a person yet.'

Lesson: We have to face the reality that there is no such thing as absolute freedom. Whether we like it or not, living in a society requires us to follow certain rules.

Miscellaneous: Other Life Truths

70. A Horse Race

The racehorse owner was very upset that his horse came in last. Not only last but way behind the rest.

Horse owner: I have not seen such a slow horse in a race in my entire life. Tan, what kind of a jockey are you? Surely you could have raced faster.

Tan: I surely could. But you know the rules. I have to be on the horse.

Lesson: It is human tendency not to blame oneself.

71. The Fox and the Goose

One day, a fox met a goose. The fox was trying to be friendly with the goose.

'Good morning, my friend,' greeted the fox. The goose quickly flew up a tree and returned the greeting, 'Good morning, Mr Fox.'

The fox continued, 'Why are you so afraid of me? Didn't you hear about the big meeting among all animals at the grand hall the other day? All of us agreed not to kill or harm each other and to live in peace. Come down and I will tell you more.'

The goose was about to fly down, when he heard and saw four wild hounds charging towards the fox. The fox ran as fast as he could.

The goose shouted, 'Didn't you say that all animals had agreed not to harm each other?' The running fox shouted back, 'But there are some who would not honour the agreement.'

Lesson: When something is too good to be true, it probably is.

72. The Revengeful Man and the Fox (Aesop's Fables)

A man was very annoyed with a fox which always disturbed his wheat field. One day, he set up a trap and caught the fox. In a fit of rage, he tied its tail with a cloth soaked with turpentine and lighted it. The fox ran as fast as it could towards a river across the wheat field to douse its burning tail. Along the way, the fire spread and destroyed the whole wheat field.

Lesson: There is a Chinese saying, 'When you plot a revenge, dig two graves.' This story aptly illustrates the wisdom of the saying.

73. The Trees and the Animals

Once, in a forest there were two trees who got very irritated with the animals running around them. They were especially annoyed with the lions which roared loudly all the time.

The two trees thought of a plan to get rid of the animals. When the animals got near them, they would shake weirdly. Soon the animals felt that the forest was becoming strange and scary. Slowly, they began to leave for another jungle.

The two trees were finally at peace. Soon the people came the know that the forest was cleared of animals, especially the wild ones like lions. They came in with their axes and chopped down the trees.

Lesson: There is a Chinese saying which goes something like, 'You are in a blessed situation, but you are not aware of it.' Your circumstances may not be perfect but they are safeguarding you.

74. Two Cats and a Piece of Cake

Two cats were quarrelling loudly over a piece of cake. A monkey saw the incident and decided to intervene. He offered to help the cats resolved their argument by suggesting that he would divide the cake into two equal pieces. He quickly borrowed a weighing scale from a nearby stall and broke the piece of cake into two pieces. He then put each piece on each end of the weighing scale. He ate a part of the bigger piece. The other piece became heavier. He then bit off a part of that piece. He ate both pieces of cake alternately trying to make them equal. Both pieces became tinier. At last, the monkey said, 'This is the best I can do. I can't divide them further. They are almost equal.' The cats also saw that both tiny pieces were about equal. They each took a piece and walked away.

Lesson: Beware of people who will take advantage of your predicament.

75. Salesmanship

An insurance agent was finally granted an audience with a wealthy businessman at the close of the day. The businessman said to him, 'Consider yourself lucky, young man, I have refused to see several insurance agents today.'

'I know,' replied the agent, 'I am them.'

Lesson: Perseverance pays off.

76. A Ring

A teacher asked her class of kids to draw a ring on a piece of paper. All, except one boy, drew a circle. The boy drew a square. The teacher asked him why. The boy replied, 'Mine is a boxing ring, teacher.'

What We Can Learn from Short Stories and Jokes

Lesson: To stand out, you have to do something different.

77. Exactly as You Asked

Andy had just shifted into his new condominium. He liked very much the wallpapers in the living room of his new neighbour. As Andy's unit was exactly the same as his neighbour, he enquired as much as he could on the wallpapers.

A week later, Andy and his neighbour met in the lift.

Neighbour: Have you completed the wallpapers in your living room?

Andy: Yes, I was left with 10 rolls.

Neighbour: It was the same with me.

Andy: Why didn't you tell me to buy fewer spare rolls?

Neighbour: You asked me how many rolls I bought not how many I used.

Lesson: Some people are just so cold and precise.

78. A Cynical Barber

Jerry was having a conversation with his barber while cutting his hair. They were on the topic of Jerry's next holiday plan. Jerry told his barber that he would be going to Country X and would visit an old classmate at the same time. The barber rattled off with all the bad things he could say about the country — crowded, polluted and dirty. He then asked Jerry which airline he would be travelling with. When Jerry told him that he would be flying with Airline Y, the barber went on to list the faults with the airline — old planes, old air hostess and not on time. Finally, when Jerry told him that he would be staying in Hotel Z, the barber rambled on all his dissatisfactions with the hotel.

One month later, Jerry and the barber met on the street. The barber asked Jerry how was the trip. Jerry replied that it had gone on quite well. The barber then asked how was the meeting with his old classmate. Jerry replied, 'The first thing he asked me was — Where did you get such a horrible haircut?'

Lesson: Some people can easily find faults with others but not so with themselves.

79. Visiting a Friend

Wife: Come with me to visit Mrs Li this Saturday. Don't worry, she'll make you feel at home.

Ricky: Then I don't think I would want to go.

Lesson: The point you used to persuade someone may work the opposite way.

80. Asking for a Pay Rise

Finally, Tony plucked up courage to see his boss for a pay rise.

Tony: Boss, I have not been given a pay rise for the last three years. Cost of living is going up. There are three companies after me. Can you kindly consider to give me a pay rise?

The boss thought for a moment. While Tony was not an exceptional staff, he had contributed faithfully to the company for more than twenty years. He did not wish to lose a loyal staff to another company.

Boss: OK. I will give you a 10% increase in salary starting next month.

Tony was very pleased as the increase was more than his expectation.

As he was about to leave, the boss asked, 'By the way, which are the three companies that are after you?'

'The electric company, the water company and the phone company,' Tony beamed.

Lesson: Find out more before you make a decision. Do not base on superficial information.

81. Seven Cows

Ricky: There were seven cows walking in a single file along a path. Which one can turn back and shout, 'I see six pairs of horns.'?

Tom: The first one, of course.

Ricky: Wrong. Cows can't talk.

Lesson: The obvious answer may not necessarily be correct.

82. The King and His Falcon (Adapted from a story from 1001 Arabian Nights)

One day, a king and his bodyguards went for a trip to the countryside. The king brought along his pet falcon. After a long walk, the king sat down at the side of a stream. His falcon leisurely circled the area. As the king was very thirsty, he took his cup and scooped some water from the stream. As he was about to drink the water, the falcon knocked off the cup. This happened several times. Finally, the king lost his patience and in a fit of rage drew out his sword and slain the falcon. Just then, a bodyguard came along and told the king that there was a very large dead cobra at the end of the stream. The king then realised that his falcon was trying to prevent him from drinking the water from the stream which could be poisoned. The king regretted that he had killed his faithful falcon.

Lesson: Words said or deeds done in a rage often end up in regrets.

83. True Tranquillity (A tale from Ancient China)

Once, there was an emperor in ancient China who was easily disturbed and agitated. One day, he said to his prime minister, 'I am easily disturbed. I frequently do not have a calm mind to handle the affairs of the state. Can you find an excellent artist to produce a painting that will calm my mind whenever I look at it?'

The prime minister commissioned three renown artists to create the painting the emperor wanted. When completed, he showed the emperor the three paintings. The first painting showed a peaceful lake amid a beautiful mountain at the background. The emperor was happy with the painting and nodded his head. The second painting depicted a moonlight on a quiet garden on a clear night. The emperor was also pleased with it and nodded his head. The third painting had a high waterfall with water gushing down. The prime minister said, 'The artist might have not understood the requirement'. As he was about to put that painting aside, the emperor interrupted, 'Hold it.

Look at it more carefully. There is a tree next to the waterfall and there is a nest on the tree. Look at how the little birds were resting calmly in the midst of the noisy waterfall. This is true tranquillity. This is the painting I want.'

Lesson: True tranquillity is not the absence of external noise. It is the presence of inner calm in spite of the external disturbances.

84. The One-year King

In a strange country, her king would rule for only one year. After the one-year's reign, the king would be sent to an uninhibited island. A council of elders would appoint a new king annually from a pool of eligible citizens. The citizen picked could not reject the appointment.

On the last day of his reign, the king would sit on a grand chair on an elephant and went around the country bidding farewell to the people. It was the saddest day for the outgoing king as after a year of living in luxury in the palace, he would have to meet the fate of being banished to an isolated island.

One day, the council picked an exceptional king. The first thing he did was to visit the island with his ministers and advisers. He saw no one living on the island. The island was a dense jungle with wild animals. All the past kings were dead, probably eaten by the wild animals. He ordered his men to get rid of the wild animals and cleared the jungle. He then devised a plan to develop the island. After nine months, the island was turned into a beautiful place. Crops grew, useful animals were brought in, and houses, a port and a park were built. Soon, people came to stay on the island and tourists visited the island.

On the last day of his reign, he also went around to bid farewell to the people. Unlike the past outgoing kings, he was not sad at all as he knew a big house was waiting for him on the island. The people saw the king's wisdom and foresight, and they made him their permanent king.

Lesson: Do what you can within your control to change your destiny.

www.ingramcontent.com/pod-product-compliance
Lightning Source LLC
LaVergne TN
LVHW091558060526
838200LV00036B/890